How Did I Get Here?

How Did I Get Here?

Tony McDowell

Matador
9 Priory Business Park,
Wistow Road, Kibworth Beauchamp,
Leicestershire, LE8 0RX
Tel: 0116 279 2299
Email: books@troubador.co.uk
Web: www.troubador.co.uk/matador
Twitter: @matadorbooks

ISBN 978 1789010 206

British Library Cataloguing in Publication Data.
A catalogue record for this book is available from the British Library.

Printed and bound in Great Britain by 4edge Limited
Typeset in 11pt Aldine 401BT by Troubador Publishing Ltd, Leicester, UK

Matador is an imprint of Troubador Publishing Ltd

This book is dedicated to my wonderful family
Ann
Emmie, Isabella and Wills
James, Jess, Archie, Rex and Buddy
Alan RIP

I would also like to thank Jock Gallagher. His help and constructive
reviews were invaluable.

THE DOUGHNUT

I 'd been to Cheltenham many times... smart shopping, fine dining, luxury hotels, but nothing prepared me for my first visit to The Doughnut, home of GCHQ.

The formidable facade of the award-winning building keeps secret the activities of more than 6,000 brilliant minds who combine with MI5 and MI6 to "keep Britain safe" from whom knows what.

What was I doing here at the heart of spookdom? Was I really about to meet the shadowy figures behind our Secret Services?

As I stood there it was all too easy to recall the exploits of James Bond in the books I had read during my youth in the back streets of Birmingham. I wondered how reality would match my imagination.

But this was GCHQ... and I had an appointment to keep. I had been briefed, and security cleared. No mobiles, no cameras, no recording equipment, and I would be searched both going in and coming out.

My own briefcase contained its own secrets, details of how my company's new computing technology and services might help in the fight against the unknown geeks who carried out cyber-attacks, some state-sponsored, some just hobbyists operating from their bedroom, and some just plain criminals, who wanted to hack into the Cheltenham computers.

Encription had now been trading for two years, although the teams' experience stretched far beyond that. Much of what we did, and had done, must remain confidential. There's a hint in the title, *Encription* (with an *i* instead of a *y* for copyright reasons).

Put simply, we combated the hackers by making sure that computer systems, and mobile devices were secure. If there had been a hacking attack or cyber fraud, we investigated it, tracked down those responsible and, if possible, provided the evidence necessary to prosecute.

The agency, along with MI5 and the Cabinet Office, had started talks with private firms because the threat posed by cyber-attacks had risen, and was rising even faster. They needed additional specialised resources who had the experience and knowledge to support their specialist teams in their fight. The companies chosen had to have demonstrable experience in preventing and tackling cyber-attacks and their work must have been to the highest standard. Their full-time, and payrolled, employees (contractors would not be considered), would have to undergo the highest level of vetting and security clearance, which would need to be rechecked on a regular basis. After all, they would be working on, and with, *Top Secret* information, often in top secret locations.

We knew we had the credentials and background. We already had the clearances and had undertaken several covert operations which GCHQ, through their National Cyber Security Centre (NCSC), were aware of. GCHQ were planning to approve a small number of organisations who, at short notice, would undertake assignments as though they were GCHQ teams.

How did I get here?

SPARKBROOK, BIRMINGHAM

I knew *she* was short of money. She always had been, even though she had been working at the same company since she was fourteen. And she was a very proficient shorthand typist. Eighteen years in the same job and still on the breadline.

She didn't see it as poverty. She didn't know any other kind of life. It was normal. Everyone else was in the same boat.

It was just that some coped better than others.

I never knew how much she earned. *Why would she discuss it with me?*

I did know she smoked. And drank. They both did. Too much at times, but didn't everyone after the Second World War, especially if they lived in one of Britain's many *not-so-good areas?* Like Sparkbrook.

Sparkbrook. A suburb of Birmingham. A slum suburb further scarred by wartime bombs because the BSA was a prime target for air raids.

Then, the Birmingham Small Arms Factory made rifles, machine guns and military motorcycles… for the war effort.

Sparkbrook was as the barracks of an industry.

Priestley Road, where *she* lived, was like many streets in Sparkbrook. It had a pub on the corner.

The Hereford Arms.

It was the centre of the community. It was small; the bar would be cramped with forty drinkers.

The Smoke Room was even smaller. Smoking was allowed everywhere, so why a dedicated smoke room? It had the luxury of seating... for ten people only! But drinks had to be bought in the main bar and taken through to the Smoke Room.

There was also The Outdoor: a tiny space no more than four by four and standing room only. No room for drinking. This was an early retail outlet. It had a hatch. Its main customers appeared to be children. They'd usually brought an empty bottle with a rubber stopper linked to the neck of the bottle by an ingenious, I thought, wire device.

We'd stand on tiptoes waiting for the barman to fill it up, so we could then scuttle back to the back-to-backs.

There were no inhibiting licensing laws then. Or health and safety. Nothing to get between the drinker and the beer.

Sparkbrook's favourite was mild: dark brown, almost like Guinness but not as strong. Bitter wasn't popular.

Mild and other drinks were sold through the hatch. Usually by the pint into the empty pint-plus bottle. Sparkbrook's frugal folk wanted the bottle to be full so the young bearer was always told to ask for *a pint and a stick*.

A *stick* was a very small measure. It might have filled a sherry glass but it meant the waiting drinker didn't feel short-changed.

The Hereford Arms' smoke-filled rooms were where arguments happened. Problems were shared. Tears were shed. Help was given... even if only a hug. And there was always laughter. Even in these bleak times of the early fifties.

Children were never left home alone. They were left outside the pub... usually with a bottle of Vimto – a fizzy red drink – and a bag of crisps.

They were safe and would be checked regularly.

On the corner opposite the Hereford Arms was the local shop. Almost every basic domestic need was catered for.

Credit was given. Most people paid. Eventually.

Priestley Road was about 200 yards long. Looking down it from the Hereford Arms, there were dull brown brick terraced houses on both sides of the road. There was an air of drabness and hopelessness. Even on a sunny summer day.

Cars, in varying states of repair, were parked on both sides of the road. It was impossible for vehicles using the road to pass one another.

Halfway down on the left-hand side, there was a small Anglican chapel that didn't seem to have any parishioners, although there did appear to be an occasional Sunday school.

A few doors down from the church, on the same side, was Car Lighting Services, specialists in car electrics. It never seemed right in this setting. The building was large. As wide as four of the street's terraced houses joined together.

Roller shutters were raised to let cars drive through to a very large workshop at the back. It could house ten cars at a time.

At the front was a service-and-parts counter, three steps up. In contrast to the chapel, Car Lighting Services was always busy. Even when it was closed, the children would play tag using the steps as their safe haven. The road outside became a football pitch and the closed shutter doors the goal.

Looking down Priestley Road, only the terraced houses on the right had alleyways.

These alleyways – only about fifteen yards long – led to other terraced houses at the rear.

The alleyways were dark and very narrow. Just about wide enough for a pram. Two adults couldn't walk side by side.

The front houses had two entrances. One – the front door – was on Priestley Road and the other – a gate – was halfway up the alleyway. Going through the gate, you immediately encountered the kitchen door.

If you carried on to the top of the alleyway you hit a brick wall… of yet another terraced house… and you then had to go either left or right. Whichever way you chose, it would inevitably take you into a neighbour's front or back yard, past their main entrance, their outside toilet, their tin bath hanging on a wall and usually their coal bunker too!

Continuing on, you would often find a third house terraced in exactly the same configuration.

At the bottom of Priestley Road was the Stratford Road, the main route into Birmingham city centre and, in the opposite direction, to Stratford-upon-Avon, about twenty-five miles away.

It was at the bottom of Priestley Road you could catch the famous yellow Birmingham Corporation double-decker buses into the city centre. The trip took about ten minutes. Including stops.

Her address was three-back-of-twenty-five Priestley Road, the fourth house up the alleyway. Once at the end of the alleyway, three-back-of-twenty-five could only be reached through a neighbour's yard. Avoiding the dog and cat faeces – the product of the many strays around – could be hazardous.

That alleyway had seen much over the years. It held many secrets and memories, not all of them pleasant.

They, she and he, had once argued in the alleyway and as a terrified bystander I remember trying to separate them. But the argument was too far gone.

I didn't even know what had started it. He said he was leaving her and that was it. They had both said this to each other many times before, but they never did; they just threatened to. As with many families in the area, lethargy or just plain resignation made it easier to stay.

Three-back-of-twenty-five, the terraced house they called home, did not overlook any green fields. There were no green fields to look over. It just overlooked other bleak terraced houses at the front and a small backyard with a high brick boundary wall at its rear.

You went into the kitchen directly from the backyard. The front door was never used. There was no reason that it should be. It didn't go anywhere... and offered nothing except more terraced houses.

The kitchen was small and dark with walls stained from damp, cooking and time.

The only source of hot water was a boiled kettle that got its heat from an old gas cooker with two cooking rings. The oven had stopped working long ago. It was probably dangerous anyway.

From the kitchen you went up a small step into a living room... about eight feet square. The walls had the same faded look as the kitchen. Damp patches and the staining from cigarette smoke could be seen everywhere. The faded look was emphasised by the peeling wallpaper... in contrast to the off-white plaster underneath.

One of the doors in the living room gave access to a small cupboard, which was never used. The door was pockmarked where a dartboard had once hung and the throwers' darts had missed their target... especially after a few drinks.

The only source of heat in the house was a grim little fireplace. The only sources of comfort: one small settee and a single armchair.

Against one wall there was a folding table, which when opened out almost filled the room. Maybe that's why it was never opened.

There was another small room on the ground floor. It was along a short passageway from the living room. From here, narrow stairs led up to two, even smaller, bedrooms.

The smaller ground-floor room was supposed to be a parlour...

supposed being the word! This was where Auntie Fan slept at night. During the day – *all* day – she sat in the one armchair. She ate sitting in that chair and used it as a commode when needed. She never went out. It was too difficult and she certainly couldn't climb stairs.

Auntie Fan had lost both her right leg above the knee and her husband during the war. There had been a direct hit on their house. He had died on the operating table having had both of his legs amputated.

Three-back-of-twenty-five was full with *her,* her husband, her mother Lol (Laura) and Auntie Fan (Francis).

There was also me (of whom, more anon).

So with only the two small bedrooms upstairs, Auntie Fan's bedroom downstairs (which was also the parlour), the small living room (crammed with three items of furniture) and the tiny kitchen, space was at a premium. Privacy was non-existent.

She had a brother, Stan, who was in the Navy. They had different fathers, but always seemed to get on well together. Stan was short with brown wavy hair. He and I also got on well together. He was a regular visitor, when he could get shore leave, but never stayed long.

Close by were a few small scraps of land... unused and empty except for the rubble, the result of collateral damage from earlier bombing. There were two derelict air-raid shelters that now functioned only as "dens" for the fertile minds of the local children.

There was neither space nor time for even the keenest of green fingers to develop a garden. In fact, the few gardens that existed were either too small to support cultivation or abandoned because no one was interested.

Sparkbrook was a racially mixed community, but there were no obvious tensions. Everyone got on, perhaps not socially but certainly in the spirit of a community where "good morning" was the norm. Mutual poverty can be a great leveller.

She was meticulous with money. She had to be.

Her little notebook, in which she kept track of everything to the nearest farthing, never left her side. In another life or in different circumstances she could have been an accountant; certainly a professional of some sort.

She was obviously intelligent. She completed the *Daily Telegraph* crossword every lunchtime at work and still had time to have a smoke and eat her pre-packed sandwich, made from whatever had been available that morning.

She was hard-working and trusted. She was an organiser, the one who arranged the annual coach outing to the seaside. She collected the money for it on payday every week throughout the year.

In the office she had also taken on responsibility for the "cigarette money".

It was kept securely in a locked cash box. Despite its name, I was never sure what the "cigarette money" was for. Did she or the company buy cigarettes in bulk that the staff could then buy cheaply? Cigarette-dispensing machines weren't around then. I never knew!

What I did know was what she had told me on several occasions; that her little cash box had a lot of money in it and she made sure she kept it safely under lock and key in her desk at the office.

He, her husband, was what some would describe as "a lovable rogue". Everyone liked him but he was unreliable. He would promise the Earth and mean it. And you would believe him but somehow something always came up that stopped him from delivering. At least that was his excuse. It was never his fault.

At the start of the Second World War – and having been born in Northern Ireland – he had enlisted in the Royal Ulster Rifles as soon as he could.

There was just one small problem: at sixteen he was underage. He had lied about his age. When it was discovered some twelve weeks later, he was discharged. He did not re-enlist, but I do think he signed up in the first place for genuine patriotic reasons.

Despite all his failings, he had many talents. Born in Portrush, Northern Ireland, he was a scratch golfer, self-taught as a boy caddy around Royal Portrush Golf Course. A man for the greyhounds, he had owned one in his early twenties, even though he couldn't afford it. There were many stories about *The Dogs*... stories often repeated. Apocryphal or not, I am not sure.

One involved a greyhound he owned which he knew was hot short-odds favourite. He didn't want his dog to win. There was not enough money in it, and he was very money-motivated.

There was much more money to be had in placing a bet on the dog he was pretty sure would win if his did not. His solution was to give his dog, the favourite, some lemonade on a sponge just before the race. This would bloat the dog and hence slow it down. The lemonade would be undetectable and in any case, it wasn't a drug, was it?

It worked. His dog came third and having bet on the other dog he went to collect his winnings.

As usual, they were spent that evening in the pub.

That was the story of his life as far as money was concerned: feast and famine. But he was not stupid. In his own way he was ambitious, always looking for an opportunity to make money but somehow never succeeding to the extent he envisioned.

There would be times, although few and far between, when he had a lot of cash in his pocket either by getting money upfront for some work he was going to do or having a good win on the dogs or horses. Most times, he barely had the price of a pint, never mind being able to give her any money for food.

While work was a necessity, greyhound racing was a passion and he gambled frequently.

On another occasion, he had backed his dog to win... he got it at good odds. His dog was third coming around the last bend. He suspected that this might be the case and had to either distract the lead greyhound or get the race abandoned.

The one thing he was was resourceful.

He had had the foresight to bring a large piece of meat with him and when thrown to the lead dog it had the desired effect of distracting it... and all of the other dogs.

The race was abandoned and declared null and void. He got his money back... as did every other punter.

He came to England shortly after his discharge from the Royal Ulster Rifles and that is when they met and when she, in a very short time, became pregnant. They got married as quickly as possible.

By this time he was a qualified electrician working for a small electrical contracting company. He was a good electrician and was always talking about having his own business.

Not long after he had discovered that he was going to be a father – just at the time when they needed stability – he decided to leave the security of full-time employment and start his own business.

He had no real plan and certainly no working capital. Work, however, was plentiful and mostly obtained over a pint.

He made sure he was paid for materials upfront. A shrewd business move.

The problem arose when he bought the materials on credit from a wholesaler and used the money, paid in advance "for materials", to pay off other debts that were by now pressing, but making sure he kept back enough for cigarettes and a few pints!

Providing food for the table came a poor third.

He was very generous, especially where she was concerned. Birthdays usually meant a substantial "practical" present, such as a washing machine. Labour-saving devices in the form of electrical goods were in great demand after the war.

In those days hire purchase was easy, especially since his precarious financial situation was not yet known. Credit checking agencies did not have computers, so vetting was cursory to say the least.

He would put a small deposit down and the birthday appliance would be delivered. She would be delighted... even though she often had to wait weeks for him to install it. She knew no better. It was what she expected.

When the regular payments began, or should have begun, he would make one or two payments and then conveniently forget or be unable to make any more. There were more pressing financial calls on his thin resources.

It wasn't until the late-payment letters arrived that she became aware of his "forgetfulness". That was what she initially put it down to. She, being worried about finances and careful with the little money she had, kept the payments up herself.

She might be poor but she had her dignity and morals.

That is how it had been since they first met. She knew he was unreliable and a bit of a rogue, but he could be fun, and she loved him... even though it was a roller-coaster ride with more downs than ups.

There were many times when she felt she could not take any more.

But where would she go and what would happen to her son, now at primary school?

She adored her son, as did her mother and Auntie Fan. While physical shows of affection were almost non-existent between the family, the lack of it was compensated for in the only way they knew how. He was spoiled with sweets and toys they could ill afford.

My coming into the world and growing up quickly had added to the ever-worsening money pressures. Arguments about money happened almost daily.

It was shortly after one of these rows, when there was literally no money and very little food, that she talked about the "cigarette money".

She had mentioned it on many occasions. She even had a plan.

Someone believable but unknown to the company needed to go in at the weekend, when there would only be one guard on duty. They would say that one of their relations had left her purse in a drawer and they had been asked to pick it up.

The purse would, of course, be in a drawer in the same desk where the cash box happened to be.

Here was a way I could help. I could be that person. I was not known and, at my age, believable.

The following Saturday, I caught a bus from the bottom of Priestley Road for the fifteen-minute journey. I walked around for a short time before nervously arriving at the security gate.

I had rehearsed my story over and over so I knew what I was going to say.

The guard was immediately suspicious and asked some searching questions. This was not going to be as easy as I had imagined. When he asked who my relation was I made up a name, and to my relief he seemed to accept that.

I had been to the office a few times previously for different reasons, including children's Christmas parties. I knew where her desk was, or at least thought I did.

The guard kept close to me and I became more and more nervous. I knew I could not go through with it.

It had also suddenly occurred to me that there was a fatal flaw in my plan. I didn't have a key to the desk… or the cigarette cash box… and if I had had the keys, it would have immediately linked her to the missing cigarette money.

I thought about making a run for it but by now we were on the third floor of the office block and I was not sure how to get out.

I had to be sure not to cast any suspicion on her. I went to a desk that I knew wasn't hers. Obviously I didn't know whose desk it was and to my shame, I didn't really care. Whose it was I did not have a clue. I just needed a desk with nothing in the drawers.

By sheer luck I found one... it was also unlocked. I told the guard that my relation must have been mistaken and had probably left her purse somewhere at home.

He believed me and we left together... with him making sure to escort me off the premises.

I stood on the pavement several hundred yards from the security gate, my heart still racing. I cried as I waited for the next bus. I never told anyone what I had done.

Life and arguments went on. Not much changed.

He carried on drinking too much and there was even less money coming in. But, as always, she managed her way around it.

It was a Friday, early in the evening, when she came home distraught and in floods of tears; the cigarette money had been stolen and the police called.

She said she did not know how, when or by whom it could have been stolen. It was just gone.

There were no signs of a forced entry and no signs of the cash box. Questioning focused on someone on the inside. Twenty people worked in the office and there were a number of suspects.

As the keyholder and custodian of the cigarette money, she felt *she* was the prime suspect but was adamant that she hadn't taken it.

As the days and weeks went by, the police questioning and presence in the office became less and less. There were bigger and more important crimes to be investigated, especially around Sparkbrook.

Eventually it became an unsolved petty crime and the money – substantial at the time – was never recovered.

Money seemed a little easier for a time afterwards.

SPOILED

She had always wanted a boy and she desperately wanted one with her man from Portrush. But not as quickly as it had happened and certainly not in the crowded living conditions in which they would have to bring up the child.

It would also have been better if they had at least been married first, but he was not a great one for commitment.

Her pregnancy was not easy because of pre-eclampsia. That would normally mean bed rest, but she needed to keep on working as long as she could.

It was possible that the continued drinking and smoking throughout her pregnancy had contributed but abstinence advice was not common in the late forties and willingness – by a pregnant woman who had just been through a world war – to heed such advice, even less common.

The birth, when it happened, was quick. One minute she was up and about and a few hours later she was in full labour – in the small upstairs bedroom of three-back-of-twenty-five – with her mother, Lol, and a very large midwife in attendance, who constantly demanded hot water… which came in bowls that had to be frequently replenished from a continually boiling kettle.

The gas ring in the small downstairs kitchen had never been so busy. Space in the bedroom was in short supply. Had *he* been there, which of course he wasn't, it would have been impossible to move.

I was born at eleven thirty on the night of Tuesday 26 October 1948. Everything was fine. I had the normal number of fingers and toes and a very loud voice!

For the first time in a long time, she was happy and content. She had real and tangible happiness.

Three days later, the midwife visited my, by now distraught, mother; I had not stopped crying and both of us had slept intermittently. Being in the same bedroom meant that no one, including my father, had had much sleep either.

'How has Baby taken to the breast?' was the midwife's first question. My mother said she had not tried me and had been feeding me warm sugar water for three days.

If there were antenatal clinics she did not know about them and would not have attended them anyway.

The midwife was incredulous. Her stern command was: 'Get Baby to the breast immediately.'

I stopped crying shortly afterwards.

I grew quickly. There was no question of her being a stay-at-home mother. She went back to work three weeks after having me.

She needed to work; no, she *had* to work.

So, Lol, who did not work, and one-legged Auntie Fan, who could not work, brought me up. There was never much food in the house, and little cooking was done as a result. Bread and butter and sweets for me were a cheap and easy substitute.

Lol was actually the tenant of three-back-of-twenty-five, the rent book was in her name and the cost of the rent was supposed to be shared amongst the inhabitants, but one – my father – was often unable to meet his commitment.

On my first birthday my grandmother, who had not had much formal schooling and, like her daughter, left school at a very early age, wrote this note to me:

26 October 1949

> *My darling little sweetheart, you will not understand this letter but it is your first birthday in this world of trouble and worry, and we hope that when you are a few years older you will have much happier times than your mummy and daddy. All of us, Grannie, Uncle Stan and Auntie Francis, send you a happy birthday message: it is good health, wealth and good luck in all the years before you and may you never know what sorrow is. So God bless you and guard you through your life.*

> *Happy Birthday to you from Nanny, Stan and Auntie*

Her prescience was remarkable.

My early years were largely unsupervised. I would play in the streets and on the bomb sites. The air-raid shelters were great places to escape to... and to pretend you were somewhere else.

While Sparkbrook was a poor area, it was also safe for children playing in the streets on their own. Burglary was almost non-existent, although that might have been because there was nothing to steal rather than that there were no criminals.

By the time I was six, I was almost totally independent. I often caught the bus on my own or with my friends. We went everywhere, including to the Bull Ring Centre in Birmingham.

I was never afraid. I was adventurous. My mother gave me a small amount of pocket money each week and I would run errands for neighbours in return for a few coppers. I was very careful with it and only spent it when I needed to.

Even at that age I knew I did not want to go through what my parents had gone through. I had ambition.

I had a couple of very good friends, Phillip and Johnny; we were a gang, and of course I had to be the leader.

Why we decided at the age of ten to get a train to Tamworth, about twenty miles away, I can't remember.

Perhaps it was the attraction of Tamworth Castle? Phillip had been there with his parents sometime before.

We were all into smoking, not in a big way. It was more important what we smoked than how much we smoked. At that time, *Peter Stuyvesants* were the cool cigarettes, although we had also tried *Black Sobranies,* amongst others. Phillip had taken three out of his mother's handbag when she wasn't looking.

We all felt it was time to be more adult with our smoking, and a pipe seemed a great idea. A lot of adults smoked pipes in those days.

Whilst in Tamworth, we passed a Woolworths. As there were no restrictions then as to what age you needed to be to buy tobacco, we went in with our pooled monetary resources.

With the plastic pouch of St Bruno and the pipe we had bought, we were soon puffing away in a quiet area of the castle grounds. The amount of time before I was violently sick fades into my memory, but I don't think it was very long.

I have never smoked anything again since then!

Apart from the pocket money, my mother spoiled me in different ways. I was, after all, an only child, and after her recent miscarriage and the resulting hysterectomy, she knew she could not have any more.

She had told me as soon as she found out that she was pregnant that I was going to have a brother or sister but it soon became clear that she was not gynaecologically suitable to bear children. I had been a one-off.

Like most children, I would get something in my mind that

I wanted and pestered until I got it, although I was not always successful. If I wanted something and went on long enough I usually got it. They were mostly low-cost affordable items within the constraints of my mother's budget, but occasionally there was an expensive item. In the fifties there were very few credit cards and certainly none that my mother would be eligible for, given the financial state and history of my father, which by then were in the public domain, so she would agree to pay for my more expensive needs in weekly instalments.

Some of the items I wanted, pestered about, and were bought, included an air rifle and a set of drums. Actually, it was just a snare drum and cymbal to be precise.

The most expensive thing I wanted was as a result of an advertisement I had seen at the local swimming baths where I went swimming with the school. The advertisement was for group scuba-diving lessons.

This was also around the time, the late fifties, that a television programme with Lloyd Bridges, called *Sea Hunt*, was on. I had seen it at a friend's house as we didn't have a television.

I went to the first scuba-diving lesson where the instructor spoke about what equipment would eventually be needed, which included your own aqualung. I couldn't wait and went on a mission of harassment; I had to have my own aqualung... now. Eventually I persuaded my mother to buy me the aqualung. The payments were spread over three years. It would be a struggle for her. I soon tired of the idea of learning to scuba-dive and the aqualung never saw water. Some months later it mysteriously disappeared along with the air rifle. There was only one suspect: my father.

I had been bought a bicycle a few Christmases previously, which I used a lot. The local bicycle shop at the bottom of Priestley Road was a dealer for Dawes Cycles, which was, in its day, seen as a cut above the rest. Its bikes were also very expensive. I didn't want just any Dawes bicycle; I wanted a Dawes "Red Feather", and it had to have Campagnolo shift lever gears and front derailleur brakes. It also had to be bright blue. Which meant a special order on the factory.

Dawes bikes were like very many things in those days; they were for the middle classes, but working-class folk, recognising their worth, saved up for them... a type of investment for life.

In the late forties and early fifties, English cycling club riders would very often buy factory-built bikes, brands such as Dawes, Sun, FC Parkes, Armstrong, Hercules, Hopper and Raleigh.

Dawes was always perceived as a manufacturer of bikes just a cut above the crowd... a little aloof... it traded in the middle of the market... did not attempt to sponsor a team in the Tour de France, or in the Brighton-to-Glasgow event. Dawes built excellent bikes for ladies to shop on elegantly, for ladies to keep fit on, and for tourists... and for youth hostellers... and for clubmen... bikes with a sense of integrity and an honesty of purpose... bikes for all the family.

The "Red Feather" was once again bought on credit which was not going to be easy for my mother. A small deposit was paid and weekly cash payments were made over the next two years. My mother never missed a payment, but she must have been under tremendous pressure to achieve that.

With the exception of the aqualung I did use all of the items I had persuaded her to buy me. I became a good shot with the rifle, even if it was only tin cans that were the target. Wildlife seemed to spurn Sparkbrook.

I also went for drum lessons, which were not a great success. That wouldn't be the last time that it would be obvious that I wasn't musically talented. The first was at primary school when they were choosing pupils to be in the choir; I was never one of those who was asked to "step forward".

The other time was when I won a colouring competition in *The Sunday Mercury*, a local Birmingham newspaper... I obviously had some artistic talent. The prize was an accordion and six lessons at George Clay's Music Centre on Broad Street, Birmingham.

Eight winners of the competition assembled on the first Saturday morning. We were given our accordions and the first lesson started. It all sounded fine and in tune to me. The teacher stopped us and said that someone was pressing the wrong key. I looked around, only to discover it was me. I never went back, and the accordion was sold, as were many of the other things I owned, but they were not sold by me; they just "went missing".

Although I was given pocket money and ran errands, it was never enough. I wanted more, and I would do anything for it. Was this inherent, or as a result of my environment and upbringing? It didn't matter, that was what I wanted.

I had a friend who was a few years older than me. I knew that he worked at the Birmingham Fruit and Vegetable Market and he said that he could get me a Saturday job there. It was heavy work for a young boy, especially one who was thin and didn't weigh very much.

The work involved fetching new stock from a storeroom when asked to do so and taking it to the stall, which in a busy market like Birmingham was often. The boxes containing the produce weighed a lot and it took all of my effort to carry them, but I managed it.

The money was good and far more than I had ever earned before, but I soon realised I was not cut out for manual labour. After six months I left. I knew there must be other ways of earning money and I had to find them.

SCHOOL

I didn't enjoy primary school, and regularly feigned a wide range of differing illnesses, as well as using other arguments to avoid being sent there... I could be very inventive. Daily I would be in tears and desperately trying to stop my mother going to work, which of course resulted in her being late. Being as conscientious as she was, this was the last thing she needed with all of the other pressures she had.

At the beginning she gave in. She would allow me to stay at home with Lol and Auntie Fan. It wasn't long before she got wise to me and was having none of it. I was going to school and that was that.

Even though the school was only a five-minute walk away she would take me herself... to make sure that I went through the school gates. She knew that I needed the discipline and the free school milk was a help. It was a year before my "illnesses" got better and I attended regularly, and my mother got to work on time.

Once I started going to school regularly I found I was not bad at sports, especially football. Being good at something and being recognised for it can make a big difference to how a child gets on, especially when they become accepted and acknowledged.

Although I was not tall I was never bullied, but I did get into several fights for reasons that I can't now remember. If you couldn't defend yourself amongst your peers at school and in the streets of Sparkbrook, your life could be a misery and your future bleak. Out of necessity I had learned how to fight at a very young age, but I hated it.

Things settled down, but nothing changed at home, especially where money was concerned. It soon became time for me to take the eleven-plus examination. I was in a class of thirty-eight. Looking back, I remember parts of the exam involved buying pencils and having change. The question was how much change and how many pencils. I don't remember finding it hard, but I do remember being supremely confident that I had passed.

My mother was less sure, but was desperate for me to go to a good secondary school where she felt I would get a better education. She was ambitious for me; she did not want me to have to endure the life that she had.

My father, the electrician, said that I should be able to go to work in a suit and never have to wear overalls or do manual work as he had. After my experience in the market, I couldn't help but agree with him. I should be a draughtsman, he declared. The advice regarding being able to go to work in a suit was one of the only pieces of advice he ever gave me and that I paid attention to, but it would remain with me for the rest of my life and be one of my many objectives for my future.

The eleven-plus exams and my time at primary school were finished; I would now move on to secondary school, but which one? A few weeks after I had finished the exam the brown eleven-plus results envelope dropped through the letterbox. It was a nice change for it not to be a bill. I was one of only three in the school who had passed.

Because I had passed the eleven-plus I had a choice of schools. I was going to go to a secondary school which was near where my mother worked and not too far from Sparkbrook. It was Bordesley Green Technical College. Although it was called a technical college, it was not all technical, but had technical subjects as an integral part of the curriculum. You had to have passed the eleven-plus to go there.

There was a problem, though. I needed a uniform, and that was going to be expensive. How she did it, I have no idea, but my mother scraped together enough to fully… well, almost fully, kit me out. She was so proud of my new bright-blue blazer, navy trousers and cap, as was I. It was the first time in my life that I had had a complete brand-new set of clothes that matched and looked smart… I loved the cap with its distinctive badge.

And so I started "big" school, but I wasn't going to be there long.

My mother had been trying for a long time to get us into a new house or flat away from three-back-of-twenty-five. It didn't matter where, as long as she could give me my own bedroom, which I had never had, and they could at least have sex without having to check whether I was awake or not… and often I was.

By now Auntie Fan had died and my grandmother, Lol, who had been getting more and more forgetful for a number of years, was in a mental institution with advanced dementia. So my mother had more freedom, although in her case the term "freedom" was somewhat misplaced.

They had been on the council housing waiting list for several years. The list worked on a points system according to your circumstances and the availability of accommodation.

Her points had been steadily increasing, simply due to the time she had been on the list. I was getting older, and certainly too old to share a bedroom with my parents.

Due to neglect and a changing demographic, Sparkbrook and

three-back-of-twenty-five were deteriorating quickly. This helped in the argument for a move.

She would contact Birmingham City Council Housing Department regularly, often going there in person. She would take her numbered ticket and wait for several hours for her number to be called and to speak to someone, explain her situation, and hopefully, increase our chances of getting somewhere decent to live.

In the late fifties/early sixties, a lot of new out-of-town conurbations were being developed, often referred to as New Towns. Kingshurst was one of these. Kingshurst was near Castle Bromwich and north of Solihull. It was an extension of Birmingham's boundaries and was where several new houses were being built, which was what my mother wanted.

Kingshurst had been a greenfield site before building began and the developers had tried to retain as much of the green open spaces as possible given the number of houses they were required to deliver. It was certainly a world apart from Sparkbrook.

In order to maximise space, most of the accommodation required was satisfied by high-rise blocks of flats, and high-rise meant exactly that; fourteen storeys or higher. Where there were high-rise blocks there were usually several of them. The small footprint meant that little land was used to build them, but a large number of residents could be accommodated.

Eventually we were offered a two-bedroom flat on the seventh floor of DeMontfort House, which had fourteen floors.

It was new and it would be ours. Well, at least we would be the tenants.

It was still the barracks of an industry, only the geography and surroundings had changed. Kingshurst and DeMontfort House were too far from Bordesley Technical College for me to travel daily. So I would have to change schools. I had only been at Bordesley twelve months and was beginning to enjoy it.

There were two choices: the local secondary comprehensive state school, where it was not a pre-requisite to have passed the eleven-plus to attend, and Coleshill Grammar School, where the eleven-plus was an essential requirement. Coleshill Grammar was about two miles away from our new seventh-floor flat and the comprehensive less than half a mile. I had made friends quickly since moving into the flat. All of my new friends went to the comprehensive school, so naturally that is where I wanted to go. My mother was adamant I was going to the grammar school. At the age of thirteen yet another chapter started in my life.

As usual, money was short. The move, the cost of some second-hand furniture, and the still uncertain income stream from my father were all contributing factors. I needed a new school uniform, and she could not afford one. The solution, with the agreement of the grammar school's headmaster, Tom Wilson, was that I would continue to wear the bright-blue blazer and dark-blue trousers that were the Bordesley Technical School uniform until my mother could afford a new one for me. The grammar school uniform was black blazer with grey trousers.

If you wanted to make a child feel out of place, different, not one of the crowd, just make them look different from the other children. My blue blazer did that. If I am honest I do not remember anyone making any comments, but I do remember feeling out of place. I had no friends at Coleshill Grammar, and felt very lonely and isolated. I certainly didn't want to go to school, but was too old now to get away with the "I am not well" excuse.

There was, however, another solution and it came from an unexpected source… my father.

He was working; he was not necessarily adding to the household coffers, but he was busy and he needed help with the work. I was to be that help. I had told both of them how I felt. My mother understood. She said that she would buy the correct uniform as soon as she was able, but things were tight at the moment. My father took a different view... I didn't need to go to school.

We would wait until my mother left for the office, my father saying that he would take me to school. As soon as she had gone I would change from my blue school uniform into some old clothes, which limited my choice and made things easy, as I didn't have any new ones.

I was to be his labourer, and because I was young, fit and small I was ideal for getting into tight spaces which he couldn't, especially reaching under floorboards and pulling cables through. I learnt about different types of cable and began to understand how electricity and circuits worked, at least at a rudimentary level. There was no doubt that my father was good at what he did and knew his trade. I enjoyed it and learnt a lot.

So everyone was happy. I didn't have to be the odd one out at school, my father had the help he needed, at no cost, and my mother believed that I had settled well into my new school as I seemed happy.

The school did not raise too many questions at first regarding my continual absences because I did turn up, on occasions, supported by a note of explanation from my father that I had been unwell with a recurring infection.

It all came to an abrupt halt at the end of my first term when my school report was sent to my mother. The report read:

PLACE IN FORM: *Unplaced*
It is difficult to assess his work at this stage, particularly in view of his frequent absences.

My days as an electrician's labourer were over.

At the start of the new term, after a long conversation with my mother, I began at Coleshill Grammar as if for the first time. New, correct uniform, different attitude, wanting to do well, and by now some friends.

I soon got selected for the football team and became fascinated with physics and technical drawing. Perhaps I would become a draughtsman after all.

My real passion though was languages, especially German taught by the headmaster, Tom Wilson. His wife was German and he of course spoke fluent German. Tom would often regale us with the story of his part in the war, frequently speaking in German just to make sure we were paying attention.

Tom had been a prisoner of war. As a former RAF officer, Tom Wilson was one of the organisers of the famous breakout using a gymnastic vaulting horse at Stalag Luft III – six months before it was the venue for the Great Escape.

Tom played his violin to disguise the sound of digging as prisoners practised vaulting on the wooden horse they had wheeled over to the perimeter fencing.

Little did prison guards know there was a man hidden inside the horse slowly tunnelling out of the camp. Eventually three prisoners escaped through the tunnel.

Tom remembered the ingenuity everyone showed planning every aspect of the escape with great care, even making ink for the forged documents by condensing the black smoke by burning cooking fat. Improvised tunnel lamps were made from can bases filled with cooking oil and pyjama cord was used as wicks. Bed boards and stolen planks were also used to shore up the tunnel's sides and roof.

Each prisoner given a turn to dig would pack soil back into the wooden horse before getting back in himself, covering the hole with a wooden board and covering that with the specially selected soil of a similar colour.

The horse would then be carried back to the prisoners' wooden hut where freshly dug soil would be buried beneath floorboards. The story was made into the 1950 film, *The Wooden Horse*.

Tom believed in corporal punishment and administered the

cane ("the cosh") on many occasions, but only once to me. He had a strong right arm...

Tom Wilson ran a fine school. I think we all thought him eccentric but he commanded immense respect and there were few who felt any real antipathy towards him (once the pain of "the cosh" had worn off, of course).

For his time, some of his ideas were extremely avant-garde. He introduced Russian into the curriculum twenty years before the fall of the Iron Curtain. He supervised skiing trips – an almost unheard-of activity for state school pupils in the late fifties. I never went on any of them.

I was never naturally academic. I didn't find studying easy... exams were a nightmare for me.

In some subjects where the teacher was not getting through to me, or I was just not interested, I struggled. I needed to find other ways of delivering what was expected of me, especially in maths. I needed to do it for my mother.

My answer lay in some of my new Coleshill friends who were good at the subjects that I was struggling in. I could be very persuasive when I needed to be. They didn't have a problem with me copying their homework in my weaker subjects. This was fine and resulted in me achieving an acceptable position in my coursework at the end of the term.

The problem came when I had to sit an exam and my results in those subjects were dire.

I was still driven by money. My experience of growing up without money, seeing the effect it can have and the misery it can bring, had made me obsessive about never being in that position again. I had tasted hard work when I was at the Birmingham market. I wouldn't say I enjoyed it, but I didn't mind it; I saw it as a means to an end.

Very close to our seventh-floor flat in DeMontfort House there was a newsagent and general store. We had been living in the flat for about eighteen months.

I had now settled into my schoolwork, but I knew that I had some time before I went to school in the mornings… I had no problem getting up early. I asked the owner of the newsagent if they had any paper rounds… they did. I was given the job. It meant delivering the papers twice per day, morning and evening. I had to be up at six thirty every morning and do my paper round before I changed into my school uniform and went to school.

My mother was pleased, but she insisted that when I came home from school the first thing I must do before delivering the evening papers, or doing anything else, was to change out of my school uniform and carefully hang it up. It had cost a lot of money, she said, and there was not going to be a new one any time soon.

There were other imposed disciplines including making my own bed in the morning, helping with the vacuuming, washing up and being generally tidy. These chores needed to be done before any paper rounds. Whilst they felt onerous at the time, the enforced disciplines would be a great asset to me in years to come.

It wasn't long after becoming a paper boy when the owner of the newsagent asked me if I wanted a second job serving in the shop behind the counter at weekends… of course I did.

The till was a simple mechanical one. It was constructed from polished metal, giving it a silver appearance. It had ornate designs covering it. There were only numeric keys, combinations of which, when pressed together, entered the amount of the sale. The pressing of the keys produced a reassuring clunky ring which confirmed the amount to the customer by metal tabs showing the amount popping up in a window at the top of the till.

The till would only accept a total amount and did not have the capability to add amounts together and arrive at a total. Neither was it able to calculate what change was due from a tendered amount.

Agile mental arithmetic was absolutely essential, or had to be developed very quickly. Once again that skill would serve me well in years to come.

Whilst I had more money than I had ever had, it was not enough. If I was going to be a millionaire, as I had told my mother on many occasions I would be, it was not going to be by delivering papers and working in a shop.

Coleshill had introduced me to some inspirational teachers who taught me to understand and appreciate languages, literature, physics and English; especially a visiting American teacher who brought George Orwell's *Animal Farm* to life. It was one of the first times in my life that I understood the importance of learning and what it had to offer.

As part of our German course we had to write to a pen pal, the name of whom was provided by the school. My pen pal was Eberhard Witt. We were made, by our respective schools, to correspond regularly, which we both did even though it was with faltering grammar and vocabulary in the other's native language.

Having Eberhard as a penfriend gave me the opportunity to go on a school exchange to Germany, but could we afford it? The cost of the trip was going to stretch my mother's financial resources, but I had been saving any money I had earned from odd jobs, so I was able to contribute some.

A group of about thirty of us went and I stayed with Eberhard's family. His father was a vicar and they lived in a large detached house with extensive gardens. The church was directly opposite the house.

It was accommodation, food and levels of luxury that I had never experienced before.

Eberhard had two sisters, the youngest of whom was about my age and attractive. They do say if you want to become proficient in a language, get a girlfriend from that country. My German improved greatly in a very short space of time.

Whilst on the exchange, I had met and become friendly with one of Eberhard's friends, Wolfgang. A few months after our return to England Wolfgang came to Coleshill Grammar for a month to improve his English. Wolfgang sat in on several of our lessons, and we became good friends... he was good fun and often in trouble.

Somehow, I had managed to pass enough O levels to get into the sixth form where I studied A level German and English.

By this time, I had also started learning to drive. My father had an Austin A40 saloon. It was light grey with a red interior and black roof. As part of my learning to drive, every Sunday lunchtime I was to take my father and two of his friends to a pub in Bromsgrove, a round trip of about fifty miles.

I was a confident driver and kept pestering my father to let me borrow the car and drive on my own, even though it was of course illegal. Despite all of his other roguish traits he sensibly refused, saying that it was not me that he was concerned about, but the other drivers on the road. I accepted it until the temptation became too much.

Wolfgang was due to go back to Germany, he was flying from Heathrow, and I said that I and two of our friends would take him... I would drive. We told everyone else that my father was taking him.

His flight was early on a Saturday morning and I had to be sure that my father did not miss the car. I knew that he would be out drinking locally on the Friday evening, and would not need his car. I hoped that he would also not notice that the car had gone.

The plan was that we would leave at about ten o'clock on the Friday evening, drop Wolfgang off at Heathrow, and then drive straight back so that we would be home before six the next morning. My cover story was that I was staying with a friend overnight.

I was nervous, but confident, even though I had never driven that far before. I had certainly never driven on a motorway and the M1 was a whole new experience. We successfully dropped Wolfgang off at Heathrow without incident.

We got back at five thirty in the morning. No problems. Lots of adrenalin. Great excitement. And my first real taste of true freedom and independence. The potential dangers and pitfalls in our adventure had not crossed my mind. They would simply be things to overcome if they happened.

My risky drive to London with Wolfgang had also given me a taste of what the world could offer.

Despite my poor start I was now very happy at Coleshill Grammar, until halfway through the sixth form. Even though I loved studying English literature and became fascinated by German writers such as Goethe and Schiller, my heart and ambitions were elsewhere. I needed to earn proper money and become successful.

I needed to find a job.

LOVE AT LAST

I don't remember how it came about, probably from my restlessness in the sixth form; the desire to earn proper money by finding a proper job. I started reading "Situations Vacant" in the local evening newspaper, the *Birmingham Evening Mail*.

I knew Birmingham well and I knew the Rotunda, the landmark towering circular building in the city centre. Through reading the job advertisements I discovered that on the fifteenth floor of the Rotunda was the SOS Employment Bureau. They seemed to have lots of career opportunities.

It was the winter of 1965. I didn't have an appointment and I didn't know what I wanted to do. None of the advertised positions had appealed to me.

I did have determination, so I went there, unannounced.

I had to wait some time for someone to see me. Eventually I was interviewed by a woman in her thirties and she was very helpful. It wasn't long before I had interviews lined up. The first interview was for a trainee insurance-assessor position with a large, well-known insurance company.

I didn't have a clue what an insurance assessor did, but I went anyway. There were ten of us there and we were asked to complete a written questionnaire that asked about interests, hobbies and academic qualifications. I had been playing some tennis at school and with friends, so that would be one of my hobbies.

The job sounded interesting, seemed to have good prospects and a good wage to start. It would also involve a considerable amount of training.

Having completed the questionnaire, I took it into the face-to-face stage of the interview with me. The interviewer was friendly and seemed very interested in me, asking me a lot of different questions, although as this was my first job interview ever I am not sure I was in any position to judge. After about forty minutes he explained that there were several good applicants, but that I had done well in the interview and was one of a shortlist of two.

Out of the blue he asked me to spell "tennis".

I am convinced that the reason my application didn't go any further was because I responded, 'T E N N I S S', which is what I had also written in my answers to "What are your hobbies?". It would be this simple, but devastating, rejection that would make me pay more attention to the detail of things in the future, especially spelling.

Hockley is an area about one mile to the north-west of Birmingham city centre. It was, and is, home to a large number of goldsmiths, jewellers and watchmakers, hence its name, The Jewellery Quarter. It was in the heart of Hockley that H. Samuel The Jewellers had its four-storey head office. This was where much of the manufacturing took place. It was also to be where my next, and by now fifth, interview arranged by the SOS Bureau would be. I was being interviewed for a computer operator position.

I didn't have a suit, and I didn't think my full school uniform would be appropriate. I had attended all of the previous interviews with the only smart clothes I had: a leather jacket; not biker style, more casual, but I felt smart. I did wear my school trousers. They were all I had apart from an old pair of jeans. The whole outfit was completed with my black school shoes.

The office manager, who was to interview me, was an unsmiling dragon of a woman, about fifty years of age, short and plump. Her first question was, 'Why aren't you wearing a suit?' No Christian names were used at Samuel's; it was always Mister, Missus or Miss followed by your surname. I explained that I didn't have a suit, but there was no softening of the witch's heart, and the questioning became even more aggressive. The job sounded interesting, but I left feeling dejected and resigned to yet another rejection.

The letter inviting me for a second interview was a complete shock. This time I borrowed a suit from a friend. I was a standard size and regular height at five-foot nine, so it fitted fairly well, even though it was a little loose in some parts and tight in others, but it would have to do.

This time, the data processing manager, who was responsible for the computer department, joined the interview. He was altogether much less scary than "the Dragon". At the end of the one-hour interview I was offered the position of trainee computer operator. I was shocked.

I would be paid £12 per week. I had already stopped delivering newspapers, but I didn't intend to give up my weekend working in the shop. My mental arithmetic quickly worked out that my new wage, plus the money I earned in the newsagent, would be more than I had ever earned before, and be my first real step on the road to riches. It could be the start of my financial ambitions. But was it the right move?

In my early years at Coleshill Grammar, Jim Flood had been my engineering drawing teacher. He was probably only five or six years older than I was. That's probably why we got on well together. He was also the careers master. I told Jim that I had been offered a job as a trainee computer operator, and didn't know what to do.

He then gave me advice which would change my life; I will never forget it or him. He said:

'I think computers are a thing of the future and I think that you should take it.'

When I told the school hierarchy that I was leaving because I had a job, there were mixed reactions, mostly around how I was wasting a great education and future. One teacher told me I was stupid taking such a risk when I had been doing so well in the sixth form.

I didn't care what people said. I was starting a new life, one that would mean I was never poor again. At least that was what I hoped.

I knew what I had to do. I was already self-sufficient, I had had to be. I just got on with things. I planned ahead, I was ambitious, but I always worried about what would, and could, go wrong. But providing it felt right to me, I would go ahead and do it anyway.

I was a loner. I kept my own counsel, whether they were plans, worries, or dreams. After all, I had no one to share them with.

The only thing I shared regularly with my mother was the fact that I would one day be a millionaire. She humoured me with motherly indulgence.

My mother had instilled a work ethic into me through her own example. She had also shown me, although unwittingly, how to look after money and what the effects of not having money were; which in her case had been unhappiness, continuous worry, and uncertainty. I promised myself I would never be in that position, and I knew no one could achieve that except me.

I look back now and I know that my family, especially my mother, loved me, as did my father, but in his own way. We were never a family who showed love to one another; no one was tactile, there was little affection and certainly no kissing, except on birthdays. We all just got on with our own thing, in our own discrete worlds. The only things shared openly were money worries, problems, moans and tears.

Starting work would not change this for me; in fact, it would make me, and my family, even more remote from each other, even though I was still living at home.

I started as a trainee computer operator at H. Samuel's head office in February 1966. I was very nervous. Not only was it my first full-time job, I was also doing something which, at this stage, I knew absolutely nothing about. Computers. But I was seventeen years of age, ambitious and ready for anything.

H. Samuel was an old, established company founded in Liverpool by Harriet Samuel. It had had its headquarters in Hockley since 1912.

But I wasn't at the glitzy end of one of the country's biggest jewellers. Not for me the glint of gold or the sparkle of diamonds. My first workplace was a tiny room which I was to share with a giant called the ICT 558... a machine that was to change my life. I was one step on my road to becoming a millionaire.

It didn't seem feasible at that point.

By then I had passed my driving test. I had paid for the lessons myself. My mother said that she would help me to buy a small car, on hire purchase of course. There she was again. How did she do it?

I needed to contribute something, which I was happy to do as I had been saving and was now about to start earning.

I bought a five-year-old Mini, and with it even more freedom.

At Samuel's, I worked on the second floor of the head office building in the small computer room. It was about twelve feet square, and affectionately known as the "goldfish bowl".

The computer in it was an ICT 558. ICT or International Computers and Tabulators would in time become ICL, International Computers Limited and eventually would be bought by Fujitsu.

The ICT 558 all but filled the room, leaving just enough space for a desk and two chairs.

It was housed in a large grey metal cabinet about six feet high and seven feet wide. It was a valve machine. As a result, it produced a great deal of heat. The cabinet was cooled by noisy internal fans.

The advent of the microchip was yet to come.

The 558 had to be reprogrammed every time you wanted to use it. This was achieved by feeding in the appropriate pack of forty-column punched cards. Each forty-column card contained one program instruction represented by a specific pattern of punched holes that instructed the 558 to carry out a specific instruction.

Depending on the function and complexity of the program, there would be between one hundred and a few thousand cards. As computer technology developed the different programs would be permanently held on magnetic tapes, or discs, from where they could be retrieved and run on demand; a much faster process. Feeding program cards in would become obsolete.

The industry standard at that time was eighty-column cards, mainly because of IBM and Hollerith, but ICT had inherited the forty-column card concept from its association with Powers-Samas with whom it had previously merged.

Once the program was loaded, the computer would execute each instruction in sequence and perform a pre-programmed set of actions depending on the data with which it was supplied. The data were also input via separate packs of punched cards. If the data in the punched cards were for watches then the computer operator, me, would load the program pack for watches and the program would execute the instructions which were relevant.

Samuel's ICT 558 had many different programs. They included keeping track of stock levels, placing re-orders for jewellery and watches where stock had gone below a certain level, computing individual branch analyses of sales and producing general accounts.

If anything needed to be printed out, a sales report for example, then a separate *plug board* had to be set up. The plug board was set up using a combination of wires, which as the name suggests were plugged into the plug board. The required layout and format of the printed report dictated how the wires were connected to the board.

The plug board was about six inches by twelve inches. The wires on the board were of different colours according to their function. Bletchley Park has many examples of wired plug boards.

The wired plug board, when connected to the 558, would result in more forty-column cards being punched out by the 558. The cards were then fed into one of several large, six-foot high tabulators, which stood in the main office. The relevant reports were then printed in the appropriate format.

My job was to load the correct program into the 558 and to wire the plug boards, or choose one that had already been wired, according to the next job that was to be run. After a few weeks, with some help, and many mistakes, I felt very confident.

The goldfish bowl got its name, of course, because it was in full view of the open-plan main office. The other problem with the goldfish bowl was that it could get very hot because of the heat output from the 558 and its valves.

During the summer, the 558 would often shut itself off because of overheating; there was no air conditioning, only the cabinet fans which were not that efficient.

So the answer was a large piece of cardboard and a great deal of fanning from someone. Me!

The computer input and output would not have been possible without the punched cards and the punched cards would not have been possible without the punch girls, who produced them. They used small desktop machines with keyboards that resembled a small typewriter.

The punch girls were very fast with the dexterity and speed of a good typist. It was usual for one punch girl to initially key in the data. This would produce a card with round holes. A second punch girl would then punch in the same data to the same card. Providing they had punched in the same data it would create a second hole in the same position on the card, but slightly higher, thus elongating the first hole that had been punched.

If there were a discrepancy between that which each girl had punched it would become obvious, as the final punched card would have one or more single holes, whereas they should have all been elongated.

There were other essential members of the open-plan office team, and these were "the girls" who *pulled* the punched cards. When a new item of jewellery was made, a new punched card was produced for it by the punch girls. The card contained full details of the jewellery; usually a short description, the cost and selling price, all represented by a series of elongated punched holes. There could be more than one card per item.

These stock cards, as they were known, were input to the 558 to be recorded and analysed. Once processed by the computer – my job – the cards were then sent back out to the main office where they were placed in metal racks by one of the girls.

When stock was sent out to a branch as the result of an order from the branch or a head office promotion, the appropriate punched card was pulled from the stock rack by one of the girls and once again sent to the 558 to record which branch it was now at. Once processed, the card was placed in a different rack in the office which represented the stock held at each branch. And so it went on until the item was finally sold, the appropriate card pulled, and the fact recorded by the 558. The 558 then produced, via a plug board and tabulator, a report giving a sales and profitability analysis for each branch. Another report was also produced telling the factory to make a replacement item, and the cycle started over again.

The girls who pulled the cards sat in the open-plan office in my full view, and me in theirs. There were three rows with six girls in each row.

It was a Monday morning in late July and I was busy loading a pack of program cards into the 558. I casually looked at the pullers and in the front row there was a beautiful new young girl, about sixteen, I guessed. I discovered later that she was in fact only fifteen. I was distracted the whole day and for many weeks to come.

By now I had had a few girlfriends, some of whom I thought were serious, but having seen the new addition to the pullers I knew that none of them had been like this one. I had feelings that I had never felt before, especially coming from a family where affection was never openly shown, or indeed discussed. I don't think I ever heard "I love you" spoken at home, but I wanted to utter it now from behind the glass window of the goldfish bowl.

My main feeling looking at her was one of certainty. It felt right. It wouldn't be the last time I would have a feeling of such certainty but that would be in different circumstances and not concerning love.

I couldn't concentrate and couldn't get her face and the thought of her out of my mind. The day was a blur, and very, very slow.

She was petite, I guessed about five-foot, with long, dark-brown hair. She was even more stunning the next day, Tuesday, and I was still as smitten.

I found out that her name was Ann and her mother worked in another department within Samuel's head office. Ann was still at school, King Edward's, Handsworth, and this was a holiday job, so she would be leaving after the summer holidays. I had no time to waste.

It didn't take me long to get to talk to her, just "hello" at first and then asking a few questions, to which I already knew the answers, as I had been desperate to find out more about her.

There was a party the following Saturday and I wanted Ann to come with me. But when I asked her to come to the party, she said she would have to ask her mother. Her mother said "no", because she was too young, and she didn't know me.

A setback, but not the end.

I had become persistent in almost everything I did. If I wanted something, I found a way to get it. The party did happen. She wasn't there. I knew there would be other times and opportunities.

It wasn't long before we were seeing each other almost every evening and every weekend... with certain rules laid down by her mother.

My feelings never changed. Whenever I left her I couldn't wait to see her again. Even a phone call with her created excitement and eager anticipation.

Was this love? Was I in love? Yes, I was!

I had been working at Samuel's for six months when the data processing manager called me into his office. I thought I had been doing a good job, I couldn't think what the problem was... it was my nature to think the worst. He began seriously; I expected bad news. He then told me that they were very pleased with me and wanted me to become a programmer. They were going to send me on a 558 programming course in London. I had never been to Central London. An unauthorised trip to Heathrow didn't count. I was elated and surprised, but knew that my career in computing was now really beginning.

The course was two weeks and was held at ICT's training centre in Berners Street just off Tottenham Court Road. I loved every minute of it. The only downside was that I wouldn't see Ann, so public telephones (there were no mobiles) got a lot of use.

Two weeks later and back at Samuel's in the goldfish bowl, I was now a computer programmer; well, a trainee, but I would learn very quickly. I couldn't believe that I was being paid to do something I enjoyed so much. I wanted to learn more and decided to enrol for evening classes which would give me a qualification in data processing fundamentals.

It was two nights per week for six months. I passed with distinction.

How my life had changed. I was in love. I was now a computer programmer, earning a reasonable salary. I was also even more ambitious both career-wise and materialistically, if that were possible. I was still working in the shop at weekends.

One of my ambitions was to own a British racing green MG Midget I had seen. It was only two years old and looked absolutely magnificent in the car showroom. I calculated that with my increased salary and extra hours in the newsagents I would be able to afford it. Six weeks later it was mine, or at least partly mine; the hire purchase company owned most of it.

One of my biggest thrills, and I think hers, was when I would pick Ann up from school. Hood down on the MG, a beautiful young girl in school uniform by my side and the world ahead of us, and I was only nineteen.

I had now been at Samuel's for over a year, but couldn't see where I could go from here. Samuel's computer systems remained the same. My job was mainly keeping the existing ones working; there were certainly no new system developments planned or innovative projects on the horizon.

I was ambitious and knew that technology was moving faster than Samuel's was, so I decided to see what other jobs were available. One that caught my eye was as a systems analyst programmer at Allied Bakeries. The company advertising the position was in fact a subsidiary of Allied. It was called Bradford's Bakery. Their offices were directly opposite the West Bromwich Albion Football Ground, which was hard for a Birmingham City supporter. It was also about half a mile from where Ann's parents lived in Handsworth.

I knew from my night school course that an analyst programmer not only programmed, but also designed the way the program would work and integrate within a larger suite of programs to provide an end to end, and seamless, system that worked in the most efficient way. I knew how to program an ICT 558, but that was only one of many programming languages that were used in the computer industry, so I would almost certainly have to learn a new language. I had learnt the fundamentals of systems analysis at night school; I just needed to put them into practice.

I applied and got invited for interview with the data processing manager. I would not only be programming. I would also be designing systems that would carry out stock control, order processing and accounts. Bradford's was obviously planning to make maximum use of computers in its business, including in the production process. The computer systems would run on the next generation of computer, an Elliot 803, a much more powerful processor and a larger memory than the 558. No valves. No punched cards, but there was punched paper tape, simply a slightly more efficient alternative to punched cards. There was also a printer connected. And I would indeed need to learn new programming languages.

To produce the bread and cakes, Bradford's worked twenty-four-seven, so computer systems and their reliability were paramount. If the orders were not processed on time by the computer, then bread and cakes were not made, no deliveries happened, commissions were not earned by the salespeople and profits were affected. The computer and its programs were critical.

I thought that the interview went well. I was confident that I would get the job. All I could do was wait. Two days after the interview I took Ann with me, to show her where "I would be working". A week later I got the rejection letter. I was devastated and determined at the same time. For the second time in my life I had that feeling of certainty. I would have that job.

By telephoning the receptionist at Bradford's I found out the name of the managing director, and I wrote to him. The letter was straight to the point and what I really believed. It explained that I had been for an interview with the data processing manager and had been rejected. I said that I believed they were making a mistake by rejecting me, and then said why. I said I knew that I had a lot to learn, but was willing to do so. I would work all of the hours necessary to achieve that goal and meet their expectations. All I needed was to be given a chance.

Three days later I received a letter from the managing director thanking me for my letter and inviting me back for another interview.

Four weeks later I left Samuel's and joined Bradford's as a computer analyst programmer.

I worked long hours and learnt a lot quickly. At Samuel's I had been taught to program in a language only used by the 558; it was a form of Machine Code. Machine Code programs are written in the equivalent of binary where only a pattern of zeros or ones is used. These are readily interpreted and executable by an electronic computer which only understands one of two binary states, "on (1)" or "off (0)", so I was very used to working with, and understanding, binary. Programs at this level had been entered directly into the 558 by a panel on the computer, as well as via punched cards. It was a time-consuming and inefficient process. You also needed to be very accurate in your input. If you were not, it was quite simple: the program did not work, and you would then spend a long time finding out why, or debugging it, as it was called.

It wasn't long after I joined Bradford's that they changed their Elliot 803 to an ICL 1901. This was the next generation of computers. It still used punched cards or paper tape as a medium for data transfer. The 1901 had a much larger memory than the 558 and the 803. It was also faster and more powerful in executing instructions. The 1901 had magnetic tapes which were used as a storage medium for both data and programs. The tapes were an integral part of the computer. The magnetic tapes were controlled by the computer programs.

The computer's memory was made of magnetic cores; there were 32,000 of them on Bradford's 1901. This was approximately 1,000 times smaller than one megabyte of storage today. We knew no better at the time and just worked with what we had. It ensured that you wrote programs that did what they were supposed to do using the least number of instructions possible. Having such limited memory forced you to be innovative and work out how to *instruct* the computer to do something in as few steps as possible.

Each core could hold one instruction or an element of data which, in the case of the 1901, was twenty-four binary digits in size. This was also known as a *Word*. ICL computers differed from IBM and most other computers of the day in that ICL computers worked in words and IBM and most of the others in bytes.

The 1901 did not use the machine code I had been used to. There were two programming languages. COBOL, Common Business Oriented Language, which was like writing in English. You would literally write "Add A to B" on a program coding sheet. Your instructions, which made up the program, would then be keyed into the computer directly or punched into cards or paper tape, which in turn would be fed into another computer program, known as a compiler. The compiler would translate the program instructions into an object program which was pure binary and hence understandable to, and directly executable by, a computer.

The other programming language was PLAN, also known as an assembler language. This was a much harder language to write and learn, but much more efficient. It required an in-depth knowledge of how the internal memory of the computer worked. After a short time I could program in both COBOL and PLAN, but PLAN was my favourite and the one I used most of the time.

Programs rarely worked first time and often did not perform as expected when being used in real life. This was nearly always solved by taking a "core dump" which showed exactly what state the computer memory had been in when the program failed. The problem was that the dump was totally unintelligible unless you understood binary and hexadecimal notation, which I did. There were many nights and weekends when I lost track of time going through a core dump, but I loved it.

There was another programmer at Bradford's, Ed. Ed and I became very good friends. One day we were chatting about how we might go freelance as we both wanted to have our own businesses. You could earn a lot of money as a freelance programmer, but it could be precarious if work was in short supply, or you did not have the contacts to get the work in the first place.

We agreed that we would test the market by putting an advertisement in the main computer newspaper of the day, *Computer Weekly*, which was read by nearly everyone in the industry. We reasoned that between us we could manage any jobs that came. We would program in the evenings and at weekends whilst still working for Bradford's. We placed the advertisement and waited. Two days later we had a call from a company who wanted to talk to us about using our services. We had made the advertisement look as though we were full-time and had lots of resource and expertise. We discussed their requirements with them, but it became very clear that what they wanted, in terms of time and commitment, was much bigger than we could provide, so we quoted them a price which we knew they would not accept. They didn't.

There were no more advertisements, but a good lesson had been learnt; if you are going to have your own business you need to be fully committed and resourced.

Despite my working so many hours my relationship with Ann was now very serious and we were talking about marriage, even though she was only seventeen. She was clever and both she, and her parents, wanted her to go to university. Ann had decided not to because of me... because of us. Instead she became a trainee shorthand typist at IMI, Imperial Metal Industries, which was part of ICI, Imperial Chemical Industries, much, I think, against her mother's wishes.

We decided, or at least I think we did, that we would ask her parents if we could get engaged. By now her mother had left Samuel's and was working in a shop. Her father was a printer. Like everyone in those days they both smoked, her father a pipe and her mother cigarettes. They owned, together with the building society, a semi-detached house in one of the better roads of Handsworth. Ann was an only child, and it was a very loving and close-knit family with lots of relations.

It was about eight o'clock at night when we came into the small sitting room which smelled of cigarette and pipe smoke. The gas fire was fully on – it was sweltering – which didn't help when I was already nervous. Her mother lay stretched out on the sofa and her father sat in the armchair.

I started hesitantly, 'I have something to ask you'. They were immediately wary, her mother did not move, but I could clearly see her facial expression, which gave nothing away.

I continued, 'Ann and I would like to get engaged.' Ann's father looked at her mother and she shook her head at him to indicate "no". Perhaps I should have taken more time to prepare them. I had just asked if I could marry their seventeen-year-old daughter, their only child and one they idolised. The age of consent was still twenty-one, so there was nothing we could do about it if they said no, and we probably wouldn't have anyway.

Her father asked if we would let them talk and think about it, but it was her mother who made the decisions. We agreed. Two days later I was back in the sitting room. They had made a decision. They said that their daughter was very young and had her education and life ahead of her. I think that her mother still hoped that she would go to university. They also pointed out that we hadn't known each other that long. All valid points, but we knew how we felt and had given it a lot of thought. They asked us to wait six months and if we still felt the same then they would reconsider. We waited, and we still felt the same.

The six months seemed to drag by, but when we asked again the answer was "yes".

Shortly after that, a wedding date of 10 June, 1970 was set. The tenth was a Wednesday. We both chose a Wednesday because we reasoned that it would be far easier to find a suitable venue and it would probably cost less. Ann would be nineteen and I would be twenty-one.

Thinking ahead, as usual, I had told Ann that I wanted children as soon as possible. I reasoned that we would both still be young enough when our children were teenagers to enjoy our life and them. Hopefully we would have a lot in common with them even then, and the energy to enjoy our child-free times together. I thought that we could be more like friends than parents and children. I hoped that by the time they "flew the parental nest" we would still be able and fit enough to enjoy life on our own.

The one thing I was determined about was that they would never experience the sort of childhood I had, and if I made a promise to them, I would keep it.

Having got the "green light" we could start planning for the wedding and saving for somewhere to live. The MG Midget would have to go. It was replaced by a very old dark-blue Ford Popular, the one which was often described as a *Jelly Mould Pop*.

Although the wedding was still over twelve months away we started house-hunting straight away. We had no preferred location when we started, but we both knew that we didn't want to live in Birmingham. Ann's parents had a small weekend caravan, which I had visited on a few occasions. It was in Worcestershire between Bewdley and Stourport-on-Severn on a quiet, out-of-the-way, campsite.

Both Bewdley and Stourport were on the River Severn and a great attraction for weekend visitors, like us, from Birmingham. I liked the area, but it would be a long way from Bradford's and

West Bromwich, and the rush hour traffic would be horrendous. Nevertheless we started looking at houses in the Stourport area. I can't remember how many we looked at, but it felt like hundreds. The ones we really liked we couldn't afford and the ones we could afford, just about, were awful.

Then one Sunday afternoon we came across a new development, not far from the caravan site. It was going to be a small development with not too many houses, about thirty. The property we fell in love with was a two-bedroom bungalow, still in the early stages of construction, and it was detached. It was £4,500, a lot of money to us and more than we had planned to spend, or thought we would be able to afford. The deposit needed to secure it was £450, 10 per cent, but we were told that we could still reserve it with £50 and save the balance of the deposit over six months, which we decided to do. It was going to be a struggle, but we didn't care; we were both earning. Although I continually worried about money I was confident the future was going to be good.

Excited, we rushed back to tell Ann's parents only to be told by her mother that... *we shouldn't build our hopes up and get too excited, as anything could happen.* Just what I needed to hear. Deflated, I drove back to Birmingham; I was still living at home.

I decided to be positive and the first thing I had to think about was finding a new job that was nearer to where we were going to live and one that paid more money, so I started looking. I saw one very quickly. It was for a chief programmer, which I assumed meant some management. It was close to Worcester, which was about fifteen miles from Stourport, and the traffic would not be too bad. The company advertising the position, Morganite Crucible Limited, was using ICL computers, which by now I knew well. I decided to apply. Morganite produced crucibles, made from clay. The crucibles were used in the smelting of metal under very high temperatures. Morganite also made furnace linings that could stand very high degrees of heat.

The Morganite offices were in the heart of the country about two miles from Worcester city centre, but the main manufacturing centre was in Battersea, London. The data processing manager was actually an external consultant. By now I was getting used to interviews. I also had more than one suit and tie, and once again the interview seemed to go well.

I was offered the job and would start before we got married, so I would still be living in Birmingham with a long, traffic-laden commute, but I could live with that. It meant quite a big increase in salary; I would earn £2,000 per year, but I would also soon have a wife and mortgage to support so I needed it, even though Ann would carry on working. Until she got pregnant that is.

At last we were married. The £64-honeymoon to Italy was over and we were in our own house. Ann's parents and grandparents were very generous, especially with weekly food provisions in the early days of our marriage – a mindset from the war I guess – and when they visited they always brought some groceries. The one thing that was in short supply was furniture. We had a bed and a table and three chairs, but little else.

At Coleshill Grammar, woodwork had been compulsory, so I knew how to make dovetail and mortise-and-tenon joints. At school, my most ambitious piece had been a teapot stand, but I was confident I could build an armchair. I did. In fact, I built two. It was almost impossible to pick them up as they were so heavy, probably because I had used chipboard as the base of the seat, but with sufficiently thick sponge, covered with a material chosen by Ann, and used as seat cushions they worked admirably. With our recently purchased bed we had somewhere to sleep, and now we had somewhere to sit.

Life settled into a routine and we were happy. Money was tight. Work was going well for me and I was learning a lot, including management. Morganite had decided to increase the size of the computer department, but were going to do so by recruiting from the shop floor. Anyone who wanted to could take an aptitude test. If they passed they would be invited for interview. If they passed both they would be considered for one of the two trainee vacancies available, and they would report to me.

Two new recruits with no IT knowledge or experience were found, and I had to train them. It was difficult at first, with me being so young. They were a few years older than I was, but they were eager to learn, and did so quickly. We ended up as a good team.

It would not be long before my technical and innovative ability would be really tested. The sales force from the furnace lining division wanted me to produce a program into which they could feed different specifications of furnace lining to simulate how the linings would perform and wear over time and in different temperatures. This needed to be illustrated graphically. In this way the salespeople could show a prospective client which was the optimum, and most cost-effective, lining for their purposes.

I didn't have a clue where to start.

By this time, we were big ICL users and decided to call on them for their ideas. A consultant called Geoff came in to talk to us. He was a physics graduate and would later go on to become a multi-millionaire having joined an anti-virus software company that was eventually sold, but this was now.

We got on well together and Geoff came up with the idea of representing the furnace lining using a mathematical model against which we could run various scenarios to simulate the performance, and hence the wear, that a particular lining would be subjected to during its lifetime of varying temperatures. I grasped the idea quickly and together we refined the model until we were ready to produce the necessary program.

The calculations involved were such that there was really only one programming language we could use, FORTRAN, or FORmula TRANslation language. The problem was I didn't know FORTRAN, so I had to teach myself, and quickly. Programming languages are like spoken languages; they have rules and syntax. Latin-root languages, for instance, in many cases have common roots. In the same way, programming languages have common structures, roots and syntax, so once you know one you can generally understand and learn another. Many iterations, and late nights of FORTRAN programming later, the sales force started using my program with great success.

It was early November 1971 and work was going well. I came home late; there had been a problem with one of the programs, and I had been sorting it out. I had not been in long when Ann said, 'I think I am pregnant'. We arranged to see a doctor the next day. It was a tense twenty-four hours, but he confirmed that she was indeed expecting and the baby was due the following June.

The next few months flew by. They were a mixture of joyful anticipation, real concerns about money, especially when Ann would eventually stop working, and total fear at having another human being to look after. I had only ever had to look after myself.

I immersed myself even more in work, continuing to develop new programs and making sure that everything was running smoothly, and that my trainees, no longer trainees, were performing.

Just before Christmas, Geoff from ICL called me to ask if I would like to do lunch. In those days business lunches were the norm and usually consisted of a couple of pints, but I very rarely did lunch. Although I was earning a reasonable wage our costs had gone up considerably. We had moved into our first home which was of course unfurnished, apart from my handmade armchairs, so we had had to buy a washing machine and vacuum cleaner, as well as having all of the other basic costs of running a house, which of course neither of us had had to pay for before. We then needed enough money for the mortgage. We went out rarely, so the offer of a free lunch was attractive.

Geoff and I caught up on all the gossip and compared notes on the new technologies coming through; ICL had recently introduced some new computers and technology.

Out of the blue Geoff asked me if I would be interested in working for ICL. I would be based in Birmingham, but would travel to clients all over the Midlands providing technical support and IT consultancy. I would be given a lot of training and most importantly would earn more money. I said that I would be interested.

The interview was arranged for early in January 1972. I started at ICL Birmingham in the February.

It wasn't long before I went on my first course. All ICL training courses were carried out at ICL Beaumont in Windsor, an old fourteenth-century manor house in forty acres, which at one time had been a Jesuit college. I would go to training courses in Windsor many times after that.

I travelled away a lot and became a specialist in both operating systems and programming languages, especially PLAN.

I was also involved in many of the pioneering initiatives that ICL was undertaking.

ICL was excellent at research and development, but unlike IBM, seemed unable to market it to maximum advantage. Thirty years later, virtual machines were heralded as a new innovation. They weren't.

As a result of my progress, I was not just limited to the Midlands. I had to stay away a lot, which I loved, but it was difficult for Ann, now heavily pregnant and nearly due to give birth.

Ann's pregnancy had not been easy; she, like my mother, had pre-eclampsia and being small-framed had not helped. Eventually she was admitted to hospital – for bed rest – four weeks before the baby was due. It didn't help that a week into her hospitalisation she was moved to another hospital some twelve miles away, where they had more facilities to look after cases like Ann's. The hospital was an old army barracks which had been converted. Ann hated it and cried every time I went to see her. It was heart-breaking.

I desperately wanted a girl. Eventually the day came; it was a Saturday. She went into labour, which ended up being a long one. I was dismissed to the waiting room where the only reading material was a poster on the wall detailing the Shops, Factories and Offices Act.

I was allowed in to see her after about three hours. She was in pain and was worn out... on reflection, it was probably not the best time to tell her how many urinals were needed in the workplace based on the number of staff.

I was told that the baby would not come any time soon, and that I should go home. It was about lunchtime. I arrived back for visiting at seven thirty in the evening to be told I had a daughter. I was ecstatic, but sorry I had missed the birth. We had names for both boys and girls, but when the time came none of them seemed to fit our beautiful new daughter. We had always been a little alternative, even down to putting a wall clock in a non-central position on a fireplace wall... Ann's grandmother had found it very odd and told us so. We called our wonderful little girl Emmie and I adored her.

Yet again we settled down to a new phase in our married life. We saw Ann's parents far more frequently than we saw mine. Having both been only children we found looking after a baby to be both interesting and challenging. My working as hard as I was and being away a lot did not help. The burden fell on Ann.

Life consisted of sleepless nights and nappies.

I remember the day vividly because I was back at Morganite now as the ICL expert, helping them to sort out a technical problem they had. I was in the data processing manager's office when his telephone rang. It was Ann asking if she could speak to me urgently.

My father, who was, at last, in full-time employment, had had a stroke and had been rushed to hospital. I needed to get there as soon as possible. When I arrived I was met by Ann. It was obvious I was too late. He had apparently died twice in the ambulance on the way to hospital and had been resuscitated both times, but a final cerebral haemorrhage had killed him. He was forty-nine. We knew he had not been well and had been undergoing a series of tests. The smoking, drinking and, I suspect, the stress had taken its toll.

It is amazing how many times a new life is born into a family and an existing life in that family is taken.

SOUTH AFRICA

I n ICL a salesperson earned a greater commission by selling into what was called a *competitive account*. A competitive account was one that was already using computers within its organisation, but the computers being used were not ICL ones.

The salesperson's pitch would be that the ICL computer they were proposing would work "x" times faster than their current computer… "Prove it" would be the prospect's retort.

The salesperson, of course, thought it would be easy, but it was far from it. It would mean that a very technical and innovative team of programmers within ICL would have to take a number of programs that were currently running on the non-ICL computer and convert them to run on the proposed ICL computer. And they needed to run faster. Only in this way could the salesperson's boast be proven.

The programs chosen would almost certainly be complex and in a different version of COBOL, or a similar language. Although computer languages used the same basic format and structure, there were differences depending upon which computer they were running on.

This specialist team of programmers was known as the *benchmarking team*.

I was one of the first to be seconded to the benchmarking team. We had to find and understand those differences and then change the programs so that they would run on the proposed ICL computer; a time-consuming process that often meant having to experiment and find new innovative ways of doing things.

Available computer time within ICL to carry out this type of work was also in short supply. We needed very powerful and versatile computers, which were only available in a few locations.

This meant that we would have to travel to an ICL research and development facility in West Gorton near Manchester. We worked through the night; the only time the machines we needed had spare capacity and were available.

Depending on the number and complexity of the programs, this could go on for weeks at a time, but it was really interesting work. It forced us to be at the cutting edge and try new things and new approaches all of the time.

There was, however, a cost. Because I was away so much I missed the early stages of my beautiful new daughter growing up. Ann didn't see that much of me. Although I promised it would change, it wasn't going to change anytime soon. I was enjoying it too much. I knew it could lead to bigger and better things.

I loved my family very much, but I enjoyed the freedom, challenge and innovation in what I was doing. I was selfish and hid behind the excuse that I was doing it to make sure that my child and my wife – never experienced what I – and my mother had experienced. This was actually the truth, but commitment to the job, career and money was how I was going to achieve it.

I was given more and more responsibility both technically and managerially. As part of the work I was undertaking I had been in close contact with a large, well-known consultancy that had been retained to oversee the successful implementation of a much larger project in which ICL were involved. I was working with their lead consultant on the project. We got on well together.

I was both shocked and flattered when out of the blue, they offered me a job. I was also tempted. My role would be as a technical consultant. I would earn more money, but I would also be away from home even more. I told my manager at ICL that I was considering it.

ICL increased my salary and I decided to stay.

Life was good and made even better when Ann told me she was pregnant again. Emmie was only twelve months old so Ann was going to have her hands full. I would of course be working to make sure we had the future I had promised, or was it just the future that I wanted?

James Dominic John was born on 26 November 1973.

The next eighteen months seemed to fly by, but I was once again getting itchy feet for a new challenge and, of course, more money, although I was by now earning a very good wage.

What I really wanted to do was to start my own business.

I had tried it before, but only on a part-time basis, and really without the commitment that deep down I knew it needed.

In our early years of married life, Ann had gone to a dress party. Dress parties, it seemed, were similar to the Tupperware concept. The hostess would model clothes in someone's home. A few drinks would be had and willing friends would purchase something they liked having tried it on in the comfort of a private house.

It seemed like a great idea.

It would actually be Ann who ran the parties and decided what the stock should be. I just, with Ann's advice and guidance, bought the stock from a wholesaler in the back streets of Birmingham. The dress party business did not last long, and we didn't make any money at it, but I learned a lot and it made me certain that having my own business was my way ahead.

Despite still working flat out at ICL, I decided to have another go at starting another side business. I would do anything, within reason, for money. I had seen an advertisement, placed on behalf of a major finance company, for part-time (evenings) sales people to sell second mortgages. I applied, was interviewed and offered a job. I had not told Ann that I had applied.

I would be given training which would equip me to visit people who had shown an interest and needed a loan. Which of course meant that I was at home even less having been working during the day.

I had a lot of success at it, making some large commissions, but I could never reconcile the interest rates being charged with the plight of the people concerned, as well as the fact that in many ways I felt that I was getting them into more debt, rather than helping them. My conscience was not easy, so I gave it up.

I was still only twenty-five and apart from our honeymoon in Italy, we had seen very little outside the Midlands, let alone the rest of the world.

I didn't want to leave ICL unless it was to start my own business, but that would have been too risky on a full-time basis at this stage in our lives, not to mention the fact that I didn't have enough money to take the risk.

I knew that if the right opportunity came up I would consider it. It wasn't long before one did, and it was within ICL. I applied.

It was a very technical role working on a Ministry of Defence project in Devizes, Wiltshire. The salary was an increase on my current one and I would be working on some very confidential, complex and interesting technologies. It would of course mean us moving. Having recently moved from our first house into a new one, we did not relish more upheaval so soon, especially with two young children to consider. We loved our new home and had settled in well. It was on a small development and was only a short distance from our first house. It had four bedrooms and had been the show house. It also came with the luxury of all of the show-house furniture.

Nevertheless, we thought it sensible, just in case I was offered the job, to look at properties and areas where we might live in Devizes. We knew it would be a big move and we couldn't afford to make a mistake. I went for the interview; it seemed to go well, but other options were soon to arise.

My first manager in ICL Birmingham, John, had transferred to ICL South Africa twelve months earlier and was back in the UK on a short visit. What I didn't know was that the purpose of his visit was to headhunt certain people from the Birmingham office to join his new team in Johannesburg. Unbeknown to me, I was one of those people.

It was 1975 and South Africa had apartheid.

I had lengthy discussions with John about what my role would be, what life was like in South Africa and what my prospects were.

He told me that I would work on the Gold Fields account, one of the largest gold-mining companies in South Africa, as a technical project manager. My salary would double. We would be paid a large lump sum for moving out there. The equivalent of one year's salary. My prospects would be excellent.

The only problem was it would be a permanent move. It was a one-way ticket. If it didn't work out we would have to fund our own return.

There was a lot to consider. The money was a big attraction, as was the weather, lifestyle and the cost of living. It was very low. From our research we knew that we could buy a really nice house for a fraction of the cost in the UK.

But what about Ann's parents and my mother? We were taking their only grandchildren thousands of miles away.

Two days after I was offered the job in Johannesburg I was offered the job in Devizes. What to do? Long discussions took place, pros and cons were considered. In the end Ann tearfully left the decision to me. I took the South Africa job.

Having sold our recently purchased four-bedroomed house quickly we left the UK and our tearful families in July 1975, with a promise that we would visit regularly and that they would fly over to us for holidays when we had settled.

ICL had told us that we would initially be provided with rented accommodation in Hillbrow.

Hillbrow was very close to Johannesburg's city centre. It was to Johannesburg what Soho is to London. In 1975 it was a bustling, cosmopolitan area frequented by many different itinerant nationalities. It was safe to walk down the street without fear of being mugged, which was very important when your wife and two children of three years of age and eighteen months were there during the day, on their own, whilst you were at work.

Since apartheid ended things have changed. Hillbrow is now a red-light district and almost a no-go area.

The ICL offices were in Braamfontein, a small business district, and within walking distance of Hillbrow. The offices were also very close to Gold Fields' offices in downtown Johannesburg, again a walk of about ten minutes. A walk that took me through the heart of the Johannesburg business and banking districts.

On my first day I went to the ICL office with some trepidation, but full of anticipation and looking forward to my new role as technical project manager on the Gold Fields account.

The ICL Braamfontein office was modern. It had six floors in a self-contained office block. There were about 150 other people working there. They included secretaries, technology specialists and salespeople. I was introduced to the team I would be working with, including a few old friends from the ICL Birmingham office who had also taken "the King's Shilling". By eleven o'clock, all introductions made, desk assigned, I was anxious to get started. I went into my new manager's office and he proceeded to brief me on the project I would be working on.

ICL had several government contracts in South Africa, one reason being that many of the American computer companies, such as IBM, were unable to sell to any organisation that was deemed to be supporting apartheid, leaving the way open for companies like ICL who did not have the same restrictions from the UK Government. ICL took maximum advantage of this freedom.

Barclays Bank in South Africa was a large account for ICL and it was in the process of a major upgrade of its existing ICL computers, which meant converting a large number of PLAN programs to a new programming language. As I was a PLAN expert they wanted me to be involved in the project full-time. Goodbye Gold Fields, hello programming.

Whilst I loved programming I was now far more interested in working in the new and innovative areas of computing, which Gold Fields would offer. Barclays' project was not going to offer me that.

I was furious and pointed out that I had not brought my family 8,000 miles for me to do a job which I was doing several years ago. The discussions went on for a few hours, but I was not giving in. At three o'clock that afternoon I left the office, saying I would be back in the morning, and went back to our rented two-bedroomed flat in Hillbrow.

It had not been a good day.

The next morning I returned to the Braamfontein office, making sure I arrived early. The discussions started again. Nothing had changed, they still wanted me to do PLAN programming, and that was where ICL's immediate need was. Gold Fields could wait.

At eleven o'clock I once again left the office, frustrated and annoyed. I returned to the Hillbrow apartment, meeting a somewhat surprised Ann and the children on the way.

Needless to say, Ann was very concerned about what would

happen, but she was very supportive. The same routine went on for four more days. I would arrive at the office, there would be what became even shorter discussions, but they always culminated in my saying that when they gave me the job I came out to do I would start work.

If the worst happened I would take us all back to England and get another job, or even start my own business. We still had spare cash from the sale of our house in England.

In the meantime, I was going back to Hillbrow. I met Ann and the children on the way most mornings, much to her ever-increasing consternation. After ten days ICL relented and I started as technical project manager on the Gold Fields account.

Looking back I risked a lot with my, some would say, arrogant attitude, but I knew I was right. Had I given in I would not have been happy and neither would my family. It wasn't the first time I had dug my heels in, and it wouldn't be the last.

We soon got to know the geography of Johannesburg and everyone advised us that we needed to live in the northern suburbs, which included Sandton, Northcliff and Rosebank. So that is where we started house-hunting even though we knew that it was going to be a lot more expensive than the southern suburbs which were geographically nearer the townships including Soweto.

As we were now, hopefully, staying we could use the proceeds from our house sale in the UK. It was not a lot, but enough for a substantial deposit, especially as the Johannesburg house prices were, by comparison with the UK, much lower.

Emmie and James soon got used to weekends spent house-hunting. They still complained as all children do.

Although house prices were considerably lower than those in the UK, we quickly realised that we could not afford a house of the sort that we wanted in the more established areas of the northern suburbs. In our travels we had stumbled across a new area that was just being developed, Rand Park Ridge. It had previously been veld, or grassland. It was very close to the northern suburb of Northcliff.

For development purposes Rand Park Ridge had been zoned into numbered extensions.

It was late one Sunday afternoon whilst exploring the many extensions that we found a house that we loved, and we could afford. If we had a dream house, this was it. It was a detached property on a quarter of an acre plot. It was modern. It had recently been built.

One of its many attractions was that it had a room that was called *the conversation pit*. Which was exactly as its name suggests. The conversation pit was down two steps from the dining room. It was an area about ten feet by ten feet. All around the perimeter of the area was seating. The continuous bench seating had been formed from concrete. The concrete was covered in the same carpet as that throughout the rest of the property. It was comfortable to sit on, and with a large coffee table in the middle was ideal for social gatherings. If every space were occupied, then the conversation pit would seat twelve to fifteen people. There were also three bedrooms and a large kitchen.

Outside, at the rear, there was a large brick-paved courtyard which separated the main property from a small brick building with windows. This was the servants' quarters.

Servants' quarters were standard in most Johannesburg houses. The quarters on our property had room for a single bed, a small wardrobe and one chair. There was a separate toilet and wash-hand basin. Very basic, but clean and could be made comfortable.

Three weeks later we had bought it.

Our new home was a bungalow, as most properties were in the newer areas of the northern suburbs of Johannesburg. We lived in Rand Park Ridge extension 27, the extension number giving an idea of the planned extent of development. There was no shortage of building land. We had scrubland all around us with just one house next door, so there was plenty of space to build more properties. The scrubland was prone to catching fire as a result of the heat and dry conditions of the grass on it. It was as a result of one such fire that we discovered that the scrubland was also home to several native South African snakes.

With things now settled at work we left our Hillbrow rented accommodation and moved into our new home.

As darkness fell on our first night, the electricity went off. We had no torches and two very frightened children. Our, as yet unmet, and only next-door neighbours came to our rescue. Fred was an Afrikaner and his wife, Liz, was from Newcastle-upon-Tyne. They had three children and that evening fed us and arranged for the electricity to be reinstated. We would spend many more happy days together as families. At that time in South Africa there was no television, so you made your own fun and entertainment, which generally meant playing bridge, barbecuing or eating out, and of course, drinking.

Life was good. I was enjoying the variety of work and challenges at Gold Fields. I had become heavily involved in sales support for a wide range of companies including other mining companies, providing technical input when needed, as I had done in the UK.

Over the next eighteen months I saw a lot of South Africa, visiting gold and tin mines and spending a considerable amount of time in Phalaborwa, which was in the north-east of Johannesburg, about a forty-minute flight by a DC3. It was a long and arduous drive by road.

The main language spoken in Phalaborwa was Afrikaans. ICL had sent me on a crash course in Afrikaans before I went up there, and it proved to be very useful. I had responsibility for mining clients there, the main product of the area being tin. Johannesburg was hot, but Phalaborwa was even hotter with summer temperatures rising to the mid-thirties centigrade.

It was essential to wear appropriate clothing. In my case that was a light-blue Crimplene safari suit with short trousers. Not a great fashion statement. A regular intake of anti-malaria tablets was also essential. The only flights were by an old DC3 prop aeroplane. It was, at times, a frightening experience, especially when trying to land on what appeared to be little more than a field.

I was acting as technical support for a salesman called Richard. Richard, as with most ex-pats who had gone out to South Africa, was very money motivated. It helped that he was also a very good salesman and not one to miss a trick.

He soon worked out that living in such a remote region as Phalaborwa meant that many basics such as beer, spirits, women's tights and luxury toiletries were either not available or in very short supply. If Richard failed to sell any of his clients a new computer or a computer upgrade, or even when he had sold them one, he would quite simply switch his sales pitch and try to sell them other basic goods they could not get. Taking orders for booze, tights and anything else that was in short supply, he would bring them with him on his next trip. He nearly always went by car because he had so many orders to bring with him, but for Richard it was business and business meant money.

By this time both sets of parents had visited us and we had been back to the UK once. I was busy so on a couple of occasions Ann and the children went back on their own for a short while.

It was whilst they were in the UK that I was asked if I would go to an ICL office in Maputo, Mozambique. The office was being closed down and there were concerns that there had been, and were still, problems there. My brief was to ascertain what was going on and to bring back some specific computer tapes which contained confidential data.

Since communism and Samora Machel had come into power in Mozambique, it had passed its heyday as a favoured holiday destination for white South Africans. The food and beaches were some of the best in the world. It was now dangerous. I hadn't told Ann what I was doing, or where I was going.

I landed at Maputo Airport having flown on yet another DC3 aircraft. Samora Machel was the military commander in power. It was obvious from the machine-gun carrying, body-building, black soldiers in camouflaged uniform at the airport, that the military were firmly in control.

I was stopped at customs by a large, well-built soldier speaking Portuguese; the sort you give respect to. He signalled for me to open the small case I was carrying. I did as ordered. I was then handed a form to sign, all written in Portuguese. Whilst I neither read nor spoke Portuguese it seemed obvious that it was a customs declaration, and as I had nothing to declare I signed it. After forty minutes, I was able to leave the terminal building. With some relief.

The tanks and overwhelming presence of soldiers on the streets emphasised how much the military were in control. There was no apartheid here, just raw communism and army rule.

On leaving the terminal I was, as arranged, met by someone with a large piece of paper bearing my name. As we introduced ourselves I was relieved to discover that he spoke English. He drove me to the office in his rather battered Ford over roads that were more suited to tanks. The office was deserted. It consisted of two rooms, each with a large filing cabinet and a desk.

I was only there for the day and had a flight out which was booked for six o'clock that evening, so I needed to be quick.

It soon became obvious that the office had been looted, or ransacked in revenge or by someone looking for something. Papers were strewn everywhere and there were signs of forced entry into both desk drawers. It took me most of the day to go through everything and find the tapes I needed, but eventually, at four o'clock, I was ready, with some relief, to leave. Driven by my contact, I headed for the airport.

The military presence was still obvious even inside the airport.

The terminal building, which wasn't large, was very busy. There were no signs of any flights either arriving or leaving.

Once again, I was confronted by a mountain of a soldier who, as far as I could understand from his gestures and hand signals, demanded the form I had signed earlier. I handed the form to him. He studied it closely. Using what amounted to sign language, he then demanded that I empty my pockets, and once again, the bag I was carrying.

You do not argue with someone who is much bigger than you and has a Kalashnikov rifle over his shoulder. Obviously ready for use. I did as he commanded.

It quickly became apparent that he had not seen computer magnetic tapes before. He studied them carefully, shook them, and then gave them back to me. I emptied the contents from my pockets including the few rands of South African currency I had brought in with me. It was at that point that I got the feeling that, having looked at my customs declaration made earlier, he was not happy.

He was ranting and raving. My eyes were firmly fixed on his Kalashnikov. Grabbing me rather aggressively by my arm, the soldier started to lead me away from the queue; to where, I knew not.

One man, in his fifties, a passenger I think, was standing nearby and had been watching the scene unfold. He came over and intervened. He spoke both English and Portuguese. He spoke to the soldier in Portuguese. It transpired that on the customs form I had declared that I was not bringing any foreign currency into the country, which in fact I was. My, by now, new friend persuaded the guard that it had all been a mistake; that I did not read or speak Portuguese. After more exchanges between the soldier and my new friend I was duly allowed through customs and into the departure hall for my six o'clock flight. The money was of course "confiscated", but I had avoided arrest.

The departure lounge was small, hot and cramped. The few

available seats were occupied. No refreshments were available and it was impossible to go outside as the doors were all guarded.

At eight o'clock in the evening there were still no signs of my, or any, flights. There had not been any other flights in or out that day, as far as I could tell. There were no announcements, electronic or otherwise. Eventually at ten o'clock a DC3 landed on the poorly lit runway. It was ours.

We all boarded. I counted eighteen passengers who probably all had a story to tell.

After my somewhat fraught day I boarded with much relief, but not as much relief as some. Sitting next to me on the plane was a black lady. She was probably in her late thirties. She was dressed in traditional African robes. She seemed very tense. She spoke a little English with a heavy accent, but we were able to communicate sufficiently well to just acknowledge one another.

By now I couldn't wait to get off the ground and back to the relative safety of Johannesburg. As the DC3 left the tarmac and became airborne the traditionally-robed lady burst into tears. She was almost inconsolable. It transpired that this was the third time that she had tried to escape from Mozambique. The first time she had been prevented from boarding the plane and the second time she had been seated on the plane, but two soldiers had boarded and forcibly removed her. It was then that I fully understood what freedom can mean to someone.

Ann loved the South African way of life; the weather, the lifestyle, the freedom. We both did. She often said that South Africa was where she learnt to drink. The children had really not known anything else, especially James. They could wander around safely in bare feet, with few clothes on, in the sunshine, enjoying life outdoors, especially with Fred and Liz's children next door, two of whom were of a similar age.

We had employed both a gardener, Samuel, and a live-in maid,

Joyce. Joyce lived in the servants' quarters in the yard. We had to visit the main police headquarters in Johannesburg in order to obtain a formal permit that would allow Joyce to live on the premises and work for us.

Joyce was wonderful with the children and they adored her. We treated Joyce and Samuel as part of our family.

It is easy to criticise what can be seen as exploiting apartheid and the cheap black labour which was available. The truth is that their lives and standard of living would have been far worse if they had not been employed, fed and looked after by the whites who cared.

We knew that Joyce had a boyfriend, but we made it perfectly clear that he could not stay in her room. To do so could have resulted in imprisonment for both of them and a large fine for us.

Joyce had been working for us for about six months. She was a slim girl, so it was not difficult to see that she was getting bigger. She was pregnant. We told her that we had no option but to send her home. It was the law. She begged us not to. Crying uncontrollably, she told us that things would be far worse back in her village, and her baby would die.

We eventually agreed on condition that as soon as she thought she was about to give birth she came and knocked on our door, regardless of what time of day or night it was. In this way we knew that we could help her by calling an ambulance and ensuring that she got to hospital safely. The hospital would be in Soweto, about an hour's drive away. It could be dangerous for whites to go there at any time.

It was about eleven o'clock at night when she did wake us up. We had made sure that we knew what to do and who to call when the time came. We immediately called an ambulance, but it had to be an ambulance that took only black people and it would have to come from near Soweto in the south of Johannesburg.

By the time the ambulance arrived Joyce was very far advanced in her labour, and in a great deal of pain. We thought that it would just be a case of getting her into the ambulance and off she would go to hospital. Although by now we were pretty well versed in how unfair apartheid could be, we never expected the ambulance driver to refuse to take her until we paid eleven rand. Eleven rand then was about eight pounds. To us it was a pittance, but to Joyce a lot of money. Which she didn't have. It was the difference between her giving birth to her baby there in Rand Park Ridge extension 27 without professional help and facilities, or going safely to hospital where the baby would hopefully be delivered safely and they would both be cared for.

We paid the ambulance driver and Joyce was taken to hospital, only to walk up to our front door the next day at midday, having caught two buses from Soweto with a new baby boy in her arms. She called him Oniuos and he became an integral part of our family.

For reasons we never discovered, Joyce left us about six months later to go back home to her other child who had remained in the family village whilst Joyce earned money to send back to them.

We found out some time later that Oniuos had died when he was two. He had contracted a viral infection. The infection had apparently not been treated either due to the lack of drugs or money. Probably both. Joyce was right. If she went back to her village her baby would die. But I think she meant during childbirth and not in the way he had.

We had now been in Johannesburg eighteen months and we had many friends both within ICL and outside of it. We had an excellent social life, including regular trips to Swaziland where we could gamble at the casino. Casinos were few and far between in South Africa. Swaziland was the nearest.

It was by chance that I came across a book called *Thirteen Against the Bank*. It made fascinating reading and told the story of an Englishman and his father who were both gamblers. They would gamble on anything, be it horses, football, poker or roulette, roulette apparently being the favourite.

They were familiar with, and used, the Labouchère method when gambling. The Labouchère system said that if you were on a losing streak you should double your stake in order to recoup your losses.

They had discovered what they called the reverse Labouchère method which applied particularly to roulette. The theory was that if you were on a losing streak then you should halve your stake, and if you were on a winning streak you should double your stake. Furthermore, bets should only be made on even chance options. In the case of roulette, red and black, odd or even.

I read the book twice to make sure I understood the system. It seemed to make complete sense. The father and son had tried it with a great deal of success at an English casino.

They had put together a team, including themselves, of thirteen gamblers who would all play the same roulette table. The theory behind this was that there was more chance statistically of at least one of the thirteen having a winning streak and compensating for some of the other players' losses. Reverse Labouchère seemed to work until the casino saw that they were winning a lot of money, and obviously playing a system. The casino was suffering heavy losses and had decided that it had to do something. It increased the minimum value of an even chance bet, which had the effect of increasing their capital requirements to play the system; an amount of money which they did not have with them. Their run of luck had come to an end. But the reverse Labouchère system had shown that it worked.

The pair were determined to try again, but knew this would be almost impossible in the UK as casinos could change the stakes whenever they wanted. The father had once been treated very badly by a casino in France when he had lost a lot of money. The son was determined to take as much money from the French casinos as possible as an act of revenge. They discovered that in France the stakes at a roulette table could only be changed by an act of parliament. Taking their team to France, they once again proved that their system worked, and they did indeed make a lot of money, only to be barred from all casinos in France.

I saw a money-making opportunity that could also be fun. I decide to get a team together.

Using small denomination coins, which I had got from the bank, we practised for several evenings at someone's house until we felt confident that we were ready for Swaziland. But was Swaziland ready for us?

On the first night everyone tried to be as casual as possible whilst they took their seats at the roulette table. Naively we pretended not to know one another. It wasn't long before we were winning and attracting a lot of attention, especially from the head of the casino.

Several people asked us if we were playing a system. We said no, but it was obvious we were. I thought that we should call it a night. We were in Swaziland for three days, so we could return tomorrow.

At the pool next day, we were all relaxing, but we had obviously created a stir. Once again, several people came up to us and asked what system we were playing. We said none; that we had just had a good run.

That evening we went through the same procedure; pretending that we did not really know each other, and taking our places early at the same table, but this time with a different croupier.

Our winning streaks started again. There had been some good runs, but one of the team had had an extraordinary run and needed to place a large amount of money on the next spin. The problem with the system was that you needed to be able to quickly mentally calculate what your next bet should be. In this case our player needed to bet 2,468 rand on red; being internationally owned and close to South Africa, the Swaziland casino operated in rands.

Our winning team member had two problems. He wasn't able

to work out how much to bet in a very short time, and by now the croupier was shortening the time between spins, thus putting even more pressure on all of the players. Our man failed to place his bet, thus ending his winning streak. By now we had been at the table for five hours and everyone was exhausted.

An essential part of the system is that you must play every spin, or the winning streak is broken. This means little or no drink, making the need to go to the toilet far less. Food was not allowed at the table, anyway. As a result, as well as being mentally exhausted, everyone was hungry and thirsty. It was time to call it a day. We had proven that the system worked. Everyone was talking about us. We had won a substantial amount of money between us which paid for all of our hotel expenses and we had money to take back to Johannesburg.

By 1977, two years since we arrived in Johannesburg, Emmie and James had both started primary school. Our parents had visited as regularly as they could afford. I was enjoying my role in ICL and with Gold Fields. I was happy. We had money and a good life.

Life in South Africa was an outdoor life. We would spend most of our time with friends and their children with frequent barbeques.

The Saturday was just such a day. We went to an outdoor park. Emmie was five. She had been running ahead of us and had fallen over. Not unusual for excited small children. Luckily a man nearby had seen her fall over and helped her up. When we arrived, he took us to one side. He told us he was a doctor and thought that she had had a fit and that we should take her to our own doctor as soon as possible, which, with great trepidation, we did. This resulted in emergency tests with our five-year-old darling daughter having electrodes attached to all parts of her body, including her head. The nurses had been wonderful. They had told her that she was just having curlers put in her hair, as Mummy did when she did her hair. It helped, and Emmie seemed fine, but we were distraught.

It all turned out well. There was not a problem. It appears that she had simply fallen over and in doing so had held her breath which caused a small convulsion. There was never a recurrence. We were so relieved.

ICL's growth in South Africa had been helped by the restrictions placed on many of ICL's American competitors in selling to an apartheid regime. This resulted in ICL needing a bigger salesforce. Their recruitment was hampered because having enjoyed life in South Africa and made some money, several people were moving back to the UK, thus reducing the number of potential candidates with the necessary technical background.

ICL always advertised vacancies internally first. So, when an advertisement appeared to join the sales team I told Ann I was going to apply. She was totally against it. She did not think it was a good career move and I would be taking an unnecessary risk. I had my own doubts, and whilst I was making a very good living in my current role I knew that I could make a lot more money – if successful – as a salesman.

I applied, and after several interviews, was offered the job. My major account was to be Gold Fields. I knew most people in the Gold Fields management structure and of course in the IT department, especially Mike who was the head of IT.

It was around this time that ICL had introduced a new range of computer known as the 2900 series. It was not compatible with any previous ICL machines or any other competitors' computers, but it did boast a new range of technology including virtual machines, a concept which many believe was only introduced in the nineties. ICL had it in the seventies. ICL had developed the use of virtual machines in their VME operating systems. Virtual machines are software configured as several discrete computers but use only one physical server, thus creating several new servers and saving the cost of additional physical servers. This maximises the full capacity of the one server. In normal circumstances a lot of a physical server's power and capacity goes unused and is wasted. This was in the mid-seventies, although the idea had first been muted in the sixties. I had been involved in early releases of the new technology so already had a head start.

Gold Fields was a long-time ICL user and as such was a prime target for IBM and other manufacturers. For some reason, the US Government did not see Gold Fields as promoting apartheid and therefore it was an acceptable target for US computer companies.

Its current ICL machines were due for replacement and the advent of the 2900 series expedited Gold Fields' decision to look at what was available in the wider marketplace.

This meant it would go out to tender.

So here was I, a rooky salesman who had been given responsibility for one of ICL's largest South African accounts, and for the first time in several years they decide to go to the open market.

My job was made more difficult by the fact that the 2900 was so new and there were none in South Africa that we could demonstrate the technology to Gold Fields. Those that existed were all in the UK and were not in working environments, but in research and development units within ICL and a couple of universities.

The challenge then was to sell something which was in another country, was brand-new unproven technology and was very expensive. The average 2900 in 1976 was approximately £1 million.

With my manager's agreement I flew back to the UK to see what equipment was available that I could get access to. I needed to try and put a series of demonstrations together which I could bring Mike, Gold Fields' head of IT, to. The demonstrations needed to show the sophistication and power of the 2900, and persuade Mike that the 2900 computer I was proposing was the only choice.

It was not easy, but eventually I had several demonstrations ready across several geographical computer centres. Everything was lined up and demonstration dates fixed.

On my return to Johannesburg I went through my plan with

the sales manager and the sales director, who seemed pleased. With Gold Fields' agreement the date for our trip was fixed. Mike and I would be away for about two weeks. We would visit ICL production and demonstration facilities across the UK, including a Scottish university and an ICL research and development centre in Bracknell. All we needed to do now was to book the flights and accommodation. For impartiality reasons Gold Fields insisted on paying for its own airfares and accommodation.

Three weeks before we were due to leave I was called into the sales director's office. I knew there was a problem. He was straight to the point, and very matter of fact. They had decided to send an "experienced" salesperson with Mike in my place. Whilst they respected my technical knowledge, they did not feel that I was experienced enough to handle such a large deal with potentially difficult and complicated negotiations.

The sales director thanked me for setting everything up and promised me a very good future in ICL. It was nothing personal he said. But it was to me. I was furious.

During our first two weeks in Johannesburg I had gone back to our flat in Hillbrow daily until I got what I had been promised. I was not going to give the UK 2900 trip up easily. I thought about my situation, what had been said, and what I was going to do.

I was on a one-way ticket, so returning to the UK would be at my own cost. We had sold our house in the UK. I had responsibilities and a family to support.

I sat down and wrote out my resignation. It wasn't a bluff. I was prepared to go through with it. I would go through with it. I didn't care what the consequences were. If necessary I was prepared to get another job in South Africa or go back to the UK, self-funded. I handed my resignation to my manager and left the building.

The next morning the sales director called me into his office and told me to book my ticket to the UK. I was taking Mike and I was going on my own. All I had to do now was to sell something which did not yet exist and was unproven.

The trip, whilst intensive, had gone as I had planned it, and without too many glitches. Although I had got to know more about Mike, his likes, his dislikes, his general outlook on life, I was still not sure if I was going to get the business. Mike tended to keep things close to his chest. He was giving nothing away.

After our two-week trip around the UK we were back in the Intercontinental Hotel on Park Lane in London, ready to fly back to Johannesburg in two days' time. I felt it had gone well but there were no real "buying signals".

Mike was ready to see and enjoy London and he did not mean the Houses of Parliament.

We started the evening with a drink at the bar in our hotel. We then got something to eat and had a few more drinks. Although we had now got to know one another even better, Mike had still kept the relationship very much on a business basis. As the evening went on we started sharing our past lives, what we had done and where we had been. I don't remember why, but I think Mike had said he wanted to go to Soho. At midnight we ended up in Raymond's Revue Bar. I had never been there either, so it was a new experience for both of us. It was actually a lot more luxurious than I had expected. The hostesses were very efficient. At serving drinks. The drink continued to flow.

Shortly after one o'clock two men sat opposite us; one in a dark suit, white shirt and red tie, obviously a business man, probably in his forties. The other, much more casually dressed, but in what looked like expensive clothes, was about fifty. He had well-groomed, long white hair and his face seemed familiar. On a thick gold chain around his neck he had a gold cigarette lighter. The lighter was encrusted with diamonds which were arranged in the shape of the letter R. This could only be one person. It was Raymond himself.

I didn't say anything, but Mike was studying the business man in the suit carefully. 'I used to go to university with him,' Mike suddenly declared referring to the Suit. It appeared that they had been good friends in South Africa and at university. The Suit had apparently become a well-known lawyer in South Africa and now the UK. Mike had lost touch with him when he had moved to England. With alcoholic bravado I went over to the Suit. I said that I was with Mike and he thought he knew him.

There was immediate recognition and we were invited to join both the Suit and Raymond. We did not pay for any more drinks that evening. Raymond had to leave, but before he did he took Mike and I to the box office and informed them that if either of us returned we were to get free admission and a good table.

Mike and the Suit reminisced about old times and the Suit asked Mike what he was doing in London. Mike explained that I was trying to sell him a new type of computer and we were here to look at what was on offer. The Suit then asked Mike if I had got the business. After a short hesitation Mike looked at me and said, 'He knows he has.'

Just before we had left Johannesburg for our trip to the UK, ICL had started their new financial year. A new financial year meant new sales targets and revised commission schemes. The one they had recently introduced became very lucrative once you exceeded your sales target. The more that you exceeded it, the greater the commission became. It also meant an all-expenses-paid trip for you and your partner to somewhere exotic overseas. It was known as the One Hundred Club and everyone achieving target was eligible. This year it was to be in a five-star hotel in the Canaries. The Canaries were considered exotic in 1977, especially from South Africa.

I had just achieved 300 per cent of my sales target from one sale and there were still eleven months of the financial year to go. I had never earned so much money. I was enjoying selling and was exceeding my sales targets, which meant even more money.

We had now been in South Africa for two and a half years. Ann loved it. She loved the weather, the way of life and the freedom, but I was getting itchy feet.

We had made many friends in Johannesburg, mostly at parties. Two people who became our best friends were Carole and Don Knaggs. Don also worked for ICL, but in a different area from where I worked. Don and Carole were both from London. When we first met them, they had only recently arrived.

Don and I were both ambitious and discussed on many occasions ideas we had for starting our own businesses. I now had enough money to take a risk. I thought about little else except taking that risk and "doing my own thing". I considered starting something in South Africa, but I just didn't feel there was a long-term future there for a white person and especially my family.

We had recently been back to England to visit family and whilst there I had been reading an article in *The Sunday Times Magazine* about the future of South Africa. The conclusion of this 1977 article was that the person in South Africa with the best future was a five-year-old black. How right that would prove to be.

Despite my continuing success at selling I was becoming more and more restless. My daily drive home from the Braamfontein office out of the centre of Johannesburg to Rand Park Ridge was on Hendrik Verwoerd Drive. Hendrik Verwoerd Drive was always busy at rush hour, and there were often hold-ups. I had travelled the road many times, but one particular evening as I was driving in the busy traffic, suddenly, out of nowhere, came an overwhelming feeling that I had to go back to the UK and start my own business, and it had to be now.

I had not been thinking of anything in particular; in fact, I was watching the freely flowing traffic pass by in the opposite direction. Daydreaming whilst at a standstill. I had been thinking about going back and had a loose idea as to what I might do, but as a result of this experience my mind was made up.

I had never been more certain of anything in my life, except for

Ann, of course. I was now committed to going back and starting on my own. I knew I had enough money to last me for probably two years, but I would have to buy a house and a car. The sale of the house in Rand Park Ridge would not yield much, if any, profit.

What I didn't have was any business to go back to. It was literally a case of starting from scratch, although I still had contacts in the UK who might be able to help.

When I told Ann what I wanted to do she was not happy. There were more tears than when we had left the UK. She and the children were happy in South Africa, why would she want to go back to England? We continued to discuss it at length, but my mind was made up. I couldn't explain it, I just knew that it was the right thing to do.

Six months later on 9 July 1978, we were on our way back to England.

THE START OF
SOMETHING

We moved back to the area we knew and we had left three years previously, Stourport-on-Severn.

Initially we knew that we would have to stay with parents until we found somewhere to rent. We would wait for a while, to see how things went, until we bought something.

A new primary school was due to open in September close to the house we had sold when we left. Emmie and James would go there.

After a month of searching we had found a small farmhouse to rent. It was in an idyllic location about eight miles from Stourport. It had three bedrooms, a small garden and was surrounded by fields.

In the meantime, I needed to get my new business going and start earning some money. I had had time to do a lot of thinking and planning.

The company would be called A McDowell and Associates and would provide computer recruitment, computer consultancy and computer training. I knew that this was very ambitious and I would not be able to deliver all of those services on my own, but I was starting from scratch and needed to keep my options open.

When I had previously worked for ICL in Birmingham, one account I looked after was Kwikform Limited. They had a data processing manager who was called Mike Hawthorne. He was a Black Country lad, born in West Bromwich. Mike was full of fun, a terrific salesman, and very good to his staff. As a result of this, Mike had made the Kwikform IT department commercially viable by selling its spare capacity to other local organisations.

Working together as supplier and client we had become very close friends. We would often have a few pints together and our wives and children would often join us for lunch or dinner.

Mike was a wheeler-dealer. He was one of my first calls on my return. I knew that if anyone could introduce me to business opportunities, Mike could. And he very quickly did.

The first opportunity Mike gave me was a short consultancy project for a firm of automotive engineers. I was to look at their current use of computers and produce a strategy for the next three years that would make more use of information technology in their business. At last I was running my own business. I was on my way, but I needed more assignments.

The other thing I needed was a car. I was still sure that my new venture was going to work. The automotive engineering assignment, which was now complete, had given me even more confidence. Had I been the prudent type I would have bought a small second-hand car, but that would not suit the image I was trying to create. So, I bought a brand-new red Rover SD1. On credit.

In 1978 computing was still in its infancy. A lot of companies were looking at introducing information technology, but seemed to be making little progress. My research suggested that this was because at board level, they had little to no technical awareness as to how computers could be used in their business and to what benefit.

There also seemed to be an almost Luddite attitude amongst the more mature board members who did not see any need for computers, let alone the large expenditure that would be required to install and manage them.

Having carried out some research on a company and its use of IT, or lack of it, I reasoned that I could put together a seminar that was as non-technical as possible, but would show how more use of IT and computers could enhance their organisation's efficiency, and their ability to make more informed decisions. The seminar would also give them a basic understanding of computers and the associated terminology.

I knew that it would mean a lot of unpaid research initially on my part, but if my concept was accepted the seminar would be a source of revenue and also, hopefully, establish my credibility as someone who could help them with their IT strategy.

It proved to be a successful strategy and within a very short time I had a considerable amount of work.

Whilst in South Africa, Don and I had discussed him joining me in the UK if the business proved to be successful. We had complimentary skills. Don was good at looking after projects and their finances and I was much more technical, and good at selling.

We spoke on the telephone often. Eleven months after I had started the company Don returned to England with Carole, his wife, and his two very young children. We were still renting the farmhouse so they stayed with us until they could find a place of their own.

It was agreed that the new organisation would be called McDowell Knaggs and Associates. This was later changed to MKA. As well as the finance side, Don also took responsibility for the recruitment division. I had been too busy with my consultancy and seminar projects to do anything with the recruitment side. Don took it on and very quickly turned it into an executive search company with one consultant based in Maidenhead.

Meanwhile, I developed the training and consultancy side of the business. Business is down to sheer hard work, having a vision to which you are fully committed and a certain amount of luck. Luck was on our side when we were approached by ICL UK to see if we could provide sales training for new recruits to their sales force.

ICL had decided that if they were to gain market share they needed to recruit more sales people. Their problem was that there was a shortage of sales people who understood computers and IT. ICL therefore decided to recruit from two sources. The first source was technical IT people who had never sold, but who ICL believed could be trained to sell. This had been me when I transferred from a very technical role to a sales role in Johannesburg.

The second group were sales people who had a successful track record in selling, be it dog food or brake linings, and whom ICL believed they could train in information technology and specifically the technology of ICL products.

My background was both technical and selling, and I knew the ICL product range well. Putting a course together and delivering it would not be a problem. For the next six months I was hardly ever at home. I was either in Southampton or London training non-technical salespeople about computers and how to sell ICL products. I was also training technical IT specialists how to sell computers. Because of the demand, Don and I were now spending most of our time on training and recruitment. The computer consultancy side was also busy.

I had sold some consultancy and programming to a large foundry in the Black Country. The project was now complete. They had obviously been pleased because they then asked us if we were able to provide full technical support to their IT department.

The business was growing fast in all areas and we were gaining a good reputation resulting in many word-of-mouth referrals.

It was time to take on more staff, which would include programmers and an administration person.

I had initially self-financed from my savings when starting the business. In order to grow the business Don and I had invested a further £5,000 each. From day-to-day work we were undertaking, MKA was generating an acceptable living for both of us, although I was earning far less than I had in South Africa.

Recruiting more people was a risk but with the potential we had, and could see, it was essential. We were able, through our recruitment arm, to find good candidates for ourselves. It meant we needed offices and they couldn't be too expensive. I had always been careful with money; Don was the same. So very tight control was kept on finances.

After a lot of searching we found two rooms above an undertaker's in Worcester. These would be our offices, and would be home to our new secretary and programmers. Being above an undertaker's was perhaps not the best advertisement for an up-and-coming business, but the rent was cheap and the space large.

I was, however, conscious that by offering consultancy, software, training and recruitment we were trying to be all things to all men. In some areas the high standards we had set ourselves were slipping. We needed to specialise and become good at, and known for, specific skills. The two areas I decided that we would concentrate on were recruitment and software development.

We had recruited someone to run the training division, which by now was delivering several government-funded training courses aimed at getting more mature people re-skilled and into IT. We then had to find them jobs and were measured on how successful we were at this. Whilst this business was going well, I did not see that it had a long-term future. Being dependent on government contracts, which could easily be withdrawn with little notice, was a risk I was not willing to take. We decided to sell the training arm. We soon found a buyer and now concentrated on the software and executive search sides of the business.

It wasn't long before I saw an opportunity to develop a software package. If we were going to be successful in software, two things were important. We needed to develop a package solution that could be sold over and over again, rather than writing bespoke software for different areas and different clients each time. It needed to produce contracted income. This could be achieved if the software needed to be updated regularly.

The opportunity I had seen was a tender that came out of the blue from the Institute of Environmental Health Officers. They wanted one organisation to develop a software package that could be used by environmental health officers (EHOs) when carrying out inspections on site. It would allow the officers to produce statutory and enforcement notices when they found a contravention of the environmental health laws. The software would in turn produce management reports and analyses for council managers.

The environmental health laws changed often so the software would need to be updated regularly to reflect the changes. This would mean contracted income to us for doing this.

The bidding process started with a round-table meeting for all interested suppliers, which included some very large organisations including IBM. We were, by far, the smallest company there.

The institute would provide the expertise to specify what was required and six pilot sites who would purchase the first systems. The problem was that the Institute of Environmental Health Officers would not pay anything for the initial development of the software, although the pilot sites would purchase the software when it was proven to work.

The pilots would pay a much-reduced price for the software, but in return would help in its development, and make sure that it met their needs and those of the environmental health laws. Once the software had been working successfully for a couple of months in the pilots, the Institute of Environmental Health Officers would recommend and promote it to all of its members, which was every council in England and Wales. Scotland was excluded.

It was a massive risk, not to mention investment for us, but I decided we should take it. We won the tender.

It took us nine months to develop the software and it was twelve months after that before we received any real revenue from sales, but after that it took off and we quickly became the largest supplier of environmental health software in the UK. Other software companies had tried writing their own version, but the recommendation of the institute was a massive advantage for us.

It had been a struggle, but we had managed the cash and our resources well. The executive search side of the business was also producing good results. At the end of 1981 we had thirty employees.

By now we had several clients using all of our services. One of our clients was a large group called Duport who owned foundries, a bed manufacturer called Vispring, and a computer services business. The computer services company provided computer bureau facilities to both group companies and to external clients. As a computer bureau it would process payroll, accounts and stock control applications on behalf of clients, which meant that those clients did not need their own in-house computing department.

We had delivered some technical training and recruitment for the computer services company and other group companies. As a result, we had become very friendly with two of the Duport Computer Services' directors, Frank and David.

It was March 1982 when David and Frank asked Don and me if we would join them, with our wives, for dinner one evening. We accepted. It was a pleasant evening and we had all had a few to drink when they revealed that the main reason for the invite was that they had been charged with expanding the computer services business. As a result, they wanted to buy our companies. They wanted us to sit on a new board with them and help them to grow the business.

We were both flattered and shocked, but agreed to think about it and talk further.

Both Don and I knew that we lacked experience in the higher levels of management and especially at board level. This, we reasoned, would give us the opportunity to get experience at this level as well as understanding and implementing more formal controls including monthly accounts packs. The price they offered was acceptable, especially as MKA was only three years old. It was more money than either of us had ever had before. It would be paid as an initial amount up front. If we then hit certain targets over the next year, there would be another lump sum. Three months later, Duport Computer Services Limited bought the MKA Group.

I was once again an employee.

The total would not be enough to retire on, especially as I was still only thirty-four, but it would allow Ann and I to buy a new and bigger house.

Having moved from the rented farmhouse, we had bought a modern detached house in Bewdley which was on a small estate, about three miles from Stourport. Bewdley was a small Georgian town on the banks of the River Severn. Before buying this house, we had seen another one in Bewdley that was up for sale. The Summer House. We had fallen in love with it, but at the time could not afford it.

The Summer House was in a very private location, overlooking both Bewdley town centre and the River Severn. It was approached by a long drive with a tennis court on one side. There was an octagonal tower which dated back to the 1750s. The tower was where tea, which was being transported on the River Severn, was brought to be weighed before it was loaded onto Severn trows. The main part of The Summer House had been built in the 1800s, incorporating the tower into its structure. It was on three floors and had five bedrooms. It also had two acres of land.

With some difficult bargaining the current owner agreed to take our recently purchased house in part exchange. We bought The Summer House in 1982. We knew that there was work to do. We also decided, or at least Emmie and James did, that it would be a good idea to have an outdoor swimming pool.

At this rate the money wasn't going to last long, but we would enjoy many great times and parties at The Summer House.

Duport had made it clear that it wanted to make more acquisitions and we would be an integral part of that process. Again, this was an ideal opportunity for us to grow the business and ourselves in terms of experience and business knowledge.

I knew that for me it would be no more than a stepping stone to my next venture. I had experienced being my own boss, and I liked it. I liked to be in control; the decision-making and the risk-taking. I wasn't sure how I was going to take to being an employee again, but I would find out very shortly.

There would be four board members of Duport Computer Services Limited, Don and I being two of them and David and Frank the other two.

Over the next eighteen months we did indeed learn a lot. We were now required to produce detailed monthly accounts packages and were involved in further acquisitions. As a board we had tripled the turnover of the computer services company, but I wasn't happy. I didn't like not being in control, and having to conform to, as I saw it, bureaucratic procedures and unnecessary red tape.

I suppose that part of the problem was that the Duport mentality was one of Black Country steelmakers, which had been their heritage, whereas we were into the new era of high tech and computing where we took risks and pushed new boundaries.

My mind was made up one day when I was called in by the human resources department. Apparently, they were not happy with my attitude. I had upset a few people. I knew who they were, but I saw it as putting across my point of view. I was told that I was being given a verbal warning; that I had to change my attitude or it would become a formal warning, which could lead to dismissal. In all my working life, I had never been given a warning such as this, and made even worse by the fact I felt it was undeserved. I must admit that I had no respect for the person who I suspected had instigated it.

It wasn't long before I lost interest and wanted to do my own thing again. It was all I could think about. I started planning. In the early years of MKA we had established a good relationship with our bank manager, Mike Magano. He was the old-school bank manager, who listened, got involved, took an interest, and along with us took a risk, which bank managers in the seventies and early eighties could, and did do.

Don had settled in with Duport more easily than I had, but he was still open to another venture. We made contact with Mike Magano and explained that we wanted to try and buy MKA back. All we needed, with some of our own money, was help from the bank to do so.

Duport had found it difficult handling the new breed of computer people that Don and I represented, especially me, as the verbal warning had proved. So, we hoped that they might be open to a buy-back, which they were.

In late 1984 we bought MKA back for the same amount that Duport had originally paid for it.

We now owned a company that was much more established and certainly had better controls, and as a result of what we had learned at Duport, a more experienced management team. Us.

Armed with our new knowledge as to what reporting and procedures worked and which ones didn't, we spent the next two years developing the businesses and expanding the staff. Don took care of the executive search company and I looked after the software side. I wanted to be more focussed in what we offered.

Opportunities were always coming up, some of which were easy to reject but others needed more thought and investigation. One such opportunity was the chance to acquire a technology business which was part of London Transport. It was a good IT services business with a lot of potential and hence carried a high price tag.

Financing the purchase would be much bigger than any deal we had done before. I wasn't even sure if we could raise the sort of money that would be needed. It would certainly put a strain on our own resources, both financial and manpower-wise, but I was going to give it a try.

I arranged a meeting with the person in London Transport responsible for disposing of the business. We exchanged non-disclosure agreements and had several discussions, but I quickly realised that they thought that we were too small; that we did not have the credentials, or the means, with which to make the acquisition. In short, they were not taking us seriously. I was almost resigned to walking away.

It was then that I came up with my contingency plan. I wasn't going to let such a good opportunity, and the chance to make money, pass me by. The company was going to be sold, it was just a question of to whom. All I had to do was to identify a suitable purchaser and act as an intermediary. I would introduce them to the opportunity on the basis that if they negotiated a successful acquisition within agreed parameters we would be paid a commission.

It did not take me long to identify two or three organisations that such an acquisition would suit. I didn't have any direct contacts in any of them, but after some phone calls, I soon found the right person in each.

I approached them all. Only one was interested. The organisation was part of a large American motor manufacturer who had branched out, very successfully, into IT services and now had a worldwide presence. The UK managing director and I got on well from the start. He was very interested and agreed that if I could bring the deal within an agreed price range then he would pay the commission we were asking for.

I went back to my contact in London Transport, who was selling the business, and told him that we had teamed up with a new partner. He was now much more interested in talking to us.

Six months later MKA was paid a commission of £250,000.

Both Don and I decided to treat ourselves to very expensive watches. But for me there was more to come.

Ann and I were very happy in The Summer House, but Ann had seen a large house, still in Bewdley, but the other side of the River Severn; the Welsh side as the locals called it. The house was on the edge of a nature reserve. It had stunning views over 2,000 acres of forest. It was known as Hitterhill.

Bewdley was very close to Kidderminster, which had once been the centre of the carpet industry. Being on the edge of the forest, Hitterhill had initially been a hunting lodge. It had been built by one of the carpet barons and, after extensive expansion, had eventually become his main residence back in the thirties.

Hitterhill was much larger than The Summer House. It had nine acres of land and separate stables which were large enough for six horses. Hitterhill was on the market as the result of a bankruptcy, exacerbated by a divorce, and was open to offers around £350,000.

Having visited it and been shown around, Ann fell in love with it. We made an offer of £300,000, only to be told by a very arrogant agent that he already had offers in excess of that. I pointed out that I was able to complete quickly. I knew that bridging wouldn't be a problem and I already had a buyer for The Summer House. He remained arrogant, and I withdrew the offer. I didn't want to leave The Summer House anyway.

About one month later I was driving back from the north when the arrogant agent called me. Apparently, all of his offers had come to nought. Was I still in a position to complete quickly based on my previous offer?, he asked. I told him I was, but my previous offer no longer stood. I would offer £250,000 and complete within two weeks. He was not happy. I told him my offer stood for twenty-four hours. The next day Hitterhill was ours.

I knew that Don had not been happy in his home and family life for some time. He seemed to find it all too tying and stressful; there was no other woman, he just wanted a change, and that included in the business. He wasn't sure he wanted to do it any more.

Ours had been a good partnership and had worked well. We had also made money from it, but perhaps it was time for a change? I relished making my own decisions again without reference to anyone else.

After several discussions, we agreed that we would try and find a buyer for MKA as a group. It was now worth a lot more than it had been when we had bought it back from Duport.

Two years previously we had agreed that it would be a good idea to recruit a non-executive director. We believed that such a person, with the right background, could provide an extra perspective to the running and growth of MKA, as well as providing a third, and perhaps more objective, view. Through various contacts we found a very good guy, Malcolm. Malcolm was a chartered accountant. He had been a partner in a very large accountancy practice and had a lot of experience in growing businesses. He was already a non-executive director with a well-known civil engineering company.

I decided to ask Malcolm for independent advice. His suggestion surprised me. He thought that the civil engineering group would be interested in buying MKA, but there was a condition: for whatever reason, Malcolm did not want Don to be part of it. I naively thought that would suit Don, providing there was enough money for him in the sale.

How wrong can one be? When I told Don what had been

suggested he went ballistic. He accused me of going behind his back and betraying our partnership. It was not going to be a partnership, nor indeed a friendship, for much longer.

In the end the deal did not go ahead but the whole situation had clarified things, certainly for me. After many acrimonious discussions we agreed that we would simply split the business. Don would take the executive search side and I would take the software and IT side.

We would both have the rights to use the MKA name. MKA Search and Selection and MKA Software would become separate, unrelated, companies.

Six months later, in November 1989, after ten years, we went our separate ways.

I knew that I could really grow the software business, especially in the production of new packaged software. As a result of our success in environmental health software we had also developed other packaged software for planning applications and building control; all procedures which easily lent themselves to automation. There was competition in this field but we had built a good reputation in government circles for both service and product delivery. The other advantage was that all of our software needed to be updated regularly due to changes in legislation. This meant that the councils had to have an annual maintenance agreement, which in turn resulted in contracted income for us. Creating a business that had contracted income had been one of my objectives from day one.

I called a meeting of all of the staff who now worked directly for me. I gave them the full background to what had happened and the resulting separation of the companies. They needed to know the truth and what the future held if I was to have them on board. I outlined my plans and said that it would not be easy. They were all on board and enthusiastic.

On my return from South Africa I had not hesitated to buy a brand-new car even though at that stage I had had neither business nor revenue to justify it. I had, however, had complete confidence in myself and my success. I now had the same confidence in the growth and success of MKA Software.

It was time to take even more risks.

One of my first considerations needed to be new office accommodation as we had been sharing office space with the executive search company.

We had moved from the undertaker's offices a few years previously. Our new offices were in the centre of Worcester with a sub-office in Maidenhead. Don had kept Maidenhead and I had kept Worcester, but Worcester was going to be too small for my plans.

I had been looking at potential offices for a little while and in doing so had happened upon a plot of land on the edge of Worcester. It had planning permission for offices. Could we afford to build? No, but I was going to do it anyway. Having looked at the purchase and build costs and made sure that we would be able to borrow the amounts needed, I obtained several quotes and chose one builder with whom I could work.

The new offices would give us more than twice the space we had been renting. We would also have plenty of car parking, which we had not had in the centre of Worcester, and be within easy access of major routes to motorways.

The bank, given our track record, was more than happy to support us. The work started and resulted in 5,000 square feet of office space with great parking and offices fitted with the latest technology. It was a new start, in a new environment with a great team. We recruited additional people and Ann joined the business. Whilst I was good at technology, ideas and selling, she was great at looking after the day-to-day, and especially the people. The staff loved her.

BRANCHING OUT

In Bewdley we had a circle of friends with whom we met most Friday evenings. One was the producer of *The Archers*, Jock Gallagher, another, Paul Hill, was the head teacher of a large Catholic comprehensive school and the third was a pharmacist, Mike Hadley. Mike was great company, a good friend, but somewhat eccentric. He was totally dedicated to his patients and to pharmacy. He could also see the future of technology in pharmacy management. Mike had spent hours painstakingly writing patient leaflets that were easily understandable, rather than the often complex instructions that came with the medication. These leaflets were handed to patients when a prescription was processed.

He and his business partner, also a pharmacist, Robert Hutt, were very much into using IT as part of the dispensing process, including to check drug interactions. This meant the computer system would automatically check that any prescription being dispensed did not include a drug which would cause an interaction with either a patient's existing condition or with another drug they were already taking, or about to take.

Mike and Robert felt that the patient management systems on the market were not good enough, so they decided to write their own, with Robert teaching himself programming and becoming the developer of their new patient management system. The system would of course include the printing of one of Mike's leaflets as well as the drug interaction checks and full stock control, automatically placing replenishment orders on wholesalers when stocks got below a predefined level.

The software would be marketed by a new company they had set up called Hadley Hutt Pharmacy Software. What else would you call it?

Mike would never stop talking about his new system and the progress they were making. He and I spoke on several occasions about the possibility of me getting involved. I thought that pharmacy software such as this would fit well within my plans for developing new software package ventures.

Mike may have been eccentric, but he was driven and had travelled most of the country demonstrating his "baby" to any pharmacist who wanted to see it. There were a lot of them. I am sure that most of his efforts were wasted but it had two results. It created a great deal of awareness and got Hadley Hutt its first commercial order, which would later be followed by multiple orders from one of the largest supermarket chains in the country.

By now Hadley Hutt Pharmacy Software was employing additional staff. Mike and Robert were also still running the dispensing pharmacy they had built. Most of the employees in the software business were either ex-pharmacists or had worked in a pharmacy, so they knew the business.

Growing the MKA software business through the development and acquisition of other software was an integral part of my plan, so I decided to once again talk to Mike and Robert about possible collaboration or even me buying their business.

We had several discussions but the major stumbling block was always Robert. By now their software was established, but Robert wanted to rewrite it. It seems to be a trait in programmers, even if they are pharmacists, to want to write the perfect program code. Such an objective is not achievable and is often not commercially viable.

Robert was insistent that any deal must be based on a commitment from me that he would have the funding and time to rewrite the software. It was not something to which I could agree since I had not been able to have a really close look at the software, and that would take some time. I was also not sure if the market needed it rewritten. It was selling well in its current state. Our discussions did not go any further. Any potential deal was off the table. Until about twelve months later.

Robert was a very keen motorcyclist. His passion was Harley-Davidsons, and it was a passion that would have dire consequences. He was riding his Harley with his wife as pillion when they were hit by a car. Robert was killed instantly and his wife was badly injured, but made a full recovery.

Mike was the ideas man and the salesman, but Robert was the developer and without each other the future was not good.

After a couple of months Mike and I reopened our discussions and eventually agreed a deal. MKA Software, which by now was considerably larger than Hadley Hutt, would acquire the pharmacy software business in exchange for MKA shares. No money would change hands. Mike, and Robert's widow, would be given shares in the new, enlarged MKA group. Mike would not be part of the business.

It did not take me long to get deeply involved in my new acquisition and it became clear very quickly that they had a good, sound product, which did not need rewriting. They also had great staff and some very good, high-profile clients. They had just not exploited the potential as much as it could have been exploited. It was now that my days in Duport paid dividends. I looked very closely at the finances to find there was hardly any financial control. There was a large overdraft and too much stock.

They had recently decided to start selling point of sale systems. The point of sale terminals needed to be stocked so that clients could have systems delivered and installed almost on demand. It appeared that little market research had been carried out and no business plan seemed to exist. This had been a step too far and too soon. It resulted in resource being taken off the pharmacy software to work on the point of sale product. They sold few and stocked too many. The products made little, if any, profit, and drained cash.

The first area to attack was the stock. That didn't take long. The second area was finance and the introduction of more financial controls. Getting everyone to buy into the new disciplines took longer. The team was not used to such disciplines.

I could, however, see two areas for potential growth. One was Mike's patient leaflet database that he had spent so long putting together. The second was the value of the data produced by the system. It was totally anonymous data, so it could not be tied back to an individual patient, but it was invaluable to drug companies, as it provided them with raw data as to what was being dispensed, to what demographic and how often.

Mike and Robert had been approached several times by drug companies to sell them the data, but had always refused on ethical grounds, even though all of their software competitors were selling their data. I decided we would now do the same.

There was, however, another opportunity I wanted to explore.

During my market research and due diligence, and prior to making the acquisition, I had come across an excellent drug interaction database that had been developed in Indianapolis in the States. I thought that if this were integrated with Mike's database, it would be a very powerful and unique tool which could be sold to not only other software developers but some of the larger high-street pharmacies.

I made contact with the man in Indianapolis who had developed the database and owned the rights to it. I told him of my interest. We agreed that I would fly out to meet him.

We got on well together and shared similar visions for the future of pharmacy software and in particular his drug interaction database.

I returned with sole rights to market the Indianapolis database throughout Europe, as well as being able to integrate the database into our own software.

When I bought Hadley Hutt it had never made an annual profit of more than £12,000 and had a large overdraft. After twelve months, thanks to more sales, including data to pharmaceutical companies, Hadley Hutt was on a sound footing. It had made a profit of £150,000 and had over £200,000 in the bank.

I ordered one of the first Aston Martin DB7s to celebrate.

It was around this time that a large retail chain who had over 2,000 pharmacies was looking for a new patient management system that could be used by their dispensing pharmacists in all of their branches. I knew that our now enhanced software would meet their requirements.

After a lot of investigation, I got us on the tender list. We had a provisional meeting at which I described the drug interaction database we had acquired. They were very interested and invited us to talk to them in more detail.

We found out that there were five other companies who had been invited to bid. One of them was a large American corporation based in Atlanta, Georgia, National Data Corporation, or NDC. NDC was a claims processor for blue-cross claims in America. This meant that when a claim was made for the re-imbursements of medication costs or medical treatment, NDC's system processed it and arranged for payment to the paying patient.

Whilst we felt our patient management system was the best of breed in many ways, especially at the point of dispensing, it lacked some functionality in the back-office function, especially in the stock control and accounting functions. This was not surprising as it was something that Mike and Robert saw as necessary but not top priority. The drug interactions and patient leaflets were far more important to them. NDC, on the other hand, had an excellent back-office system, but their dispensing was too Americanised and would not go down well with the average British pharmacist or patient.

The retail pharmacy group who had issued the tender had arranged a round-table meeting with all of the bidders. It was at this meeting that I got to know the two people from NDC. Over a few drinks we got on well together and were very open with one another.

After the meeting my mind was once again racing with ideas and opportunities, but my decision as to what to do next was obvious to me. I waited until the NDC guys were back in Atlanta and made contact with them. I called them and told them that I didn't think they were going to win the business because of their dispensing system and I didn't think we would win it either because of our back office. I then suggested that if we interfaced our dispensing system with their back office we could both win. They seemed to like the idea and said that they would get back to me.

About two weeks later they came back to me and said that they were coming back to the UK to talk to us. They wanted to explore our product further, and also the financial stability of our company. I said fine.

They were in the UK for four days. They seemed happy with what they had seen and with Hadley Hutt as a company. They returned to Atlanta, promising to contact me as soon as they could.

One week later I got a call. They wanted me to fly to Atlanta and meet several people. Things were looking promising and my plan seemed to be working. My main point of contact was going to be a senior executive whose name was Kevin, obviously; as it turned out, like so many Americans with Irish roots. Kevin was a very pleasant and astute businessman. In his large seventh-floor office in central Atlanta we went through the usual pleasantries and discussed the combining of our software and possible joint bid.

After an hour, he told me that NDC was looking to expand and it wanted to buy Hadley Hutt. It was also planning to buy some of our UK competitors. I was lost for words; I wasn't expecting this. He then told me how much he was willing to pay. I had an idea of the value of Hadley Hutt. After all, I had turned the business around financially and it was far more organised. Nevertheless, what was being offered was far in excess of what I thought it was worth at that time.

I had been thinking of an eventual sale of the whole group, rather than just one element of it. If I accepted I would be able to take things easy, perhaps even retire. I wasn't going to do that. NDC wanted me to stay on.

We agreed to go ahead with due diligence. The due diligence that followed was to say the least intense. It lasted over a week. It was almost twenty-four-seven. There was a team of nine advisers, all from America. Two of them were external consultants from one of the large consultancy firms. The due diligence covered all aspects of the business including legals, HR and finance.

It all went well and almost two years to the day since I had bought Hadley Hutt I had sold it and made a lot of money for myself, Mike Hadley and Robert Hutt's widow.

NDC had simultaneously acquired one of our competitors. I was to become European managing director for pharmacy software, which would include Hadley Hutt and our recently acquired competitor.

We had only sold the pharmacy software part of MKA – the rest of MKA was still ours – but part of the deal with NDC was that I could not have anything to do with MKA as, not unreasonably, they wanted me to concentrate on the pharmacy businesses. By this time Ann had been working in MKA and taking an ever-increasing role with more responsibilities, and she now became managing director.

After only six months with NDC, flying backwards and forwards to Atlanta for unnecessary meetings, not to mention the big company bureaucracy, it confirmed to me once again that I was unemployable. I wanted things done my way: to be able to implement my ideas without permission or reference; to make decisions. I knew this would not be possible in the corporate environment.

I had signed a three-year lucrative contract of employment with NDC. It consisted of a high basic salary and generous bonuses triggered by hitting performance targets. I achieved all of my targets in the first nine months, and the bonus was paid.

It became obvious to me that I wasn't going to last the three years, and if I was it would not be a happy time for anyone.

Twelve months later my problem was solved, by NDC themselves. They wanted to terminate my contract. They could obviously see it wasn't working between us. That was fine with me providing they honoured my contract including the ongoing bonus element. After some discussions they agreed. My contract and annual bonus would be paid as per the original contract. I was a free man.

MORE OPPORTUNITIES

I had been out of the really technical side of IT for some time. I had a lot of time on my hands, and money in the bank. I decided to update my skills, which I did at my home desktop. It was good to be immersed once more in the detail of technology. A lot had changed.

I didn't get involved in MKA, even though I was now free to do so. Ann was doing an excellent job without me, but I was not planning to spend the rest of my life sitting at home and playing with a desktop computer.

One of the risks with suddenly having a lot of money, having sold a business, is that you can believe you have "the Golden Touch"; that you have a formula for business success. There is also the greed syndrome where you want more. This can cloud your normally cautious approach to investing. You can't just be sensible and invest in a good, boring, interest-earning account. You can do more with your money than that. After all, that is what you are good at.

The dot-com boom was in full flow, and there were plenty of

dot-com opportunities for investment. Information technology was what I knew and understood.

I had been contacted by someone I had done business with a few years previously. He said that he had been talking to two people who wanted to start an online recruitment business. They needed investment. In 1998 the concept of online recruitment was still novel.

Their idea was simple. Candidates would upload their CVs to the website. There was no charge to the candidate. Potential employers paid an initial registration fee, and a search fee every time they wanted to interrogate the candidate database for CVs that matched their criteria.

Having been part of the executive search and recruitment scene through MKA, I had always cringed at the size of the fees we charged: usually one third of the person's salary when they were placed. I felt that there must be a better pricing model that would generate higher volume and more effective results. This looked like it could be the one.

We arranged a meeting in Manchester. They were already working in the recruitment business and had raised £200,000 from three other investors. They were looking for a further investment of £100,000. The business model looked good and well researched. The fact that there were already other investors was encouraging.

I was interested, but wanted to know more, especially about them. The one question I wanted answered was, how much were they going to pay themselves? The response I wanted was as little as possible until the business had proven itself and was producing good revenues and eventually profit. I knew it would make a loss in the early months.

When they responded that they were going to pay themselves £80,000 each per year, alarm bells rang, and I should have walked out there and then. They argued that they knew the business well. They had a proven track record in it. The software was already developed.

They further argued that they had families and certain financial commitments. They said they couldn't work for any less. Greed and stupidity kicked in and I invested.

We had regular meetings in the first two months, but when I heard that one of them had flown to New York to attend a three-day investment conference, all paid for by the company, I got even more nervous, not to mention annoyed that investment money had been spent in such a frivolous manner and without consultation. This was compounded by the fact that the recruitment site was now up and running, but missing its targets by a mile.

After six months the inevitable happened. They said that without further investment the business would fold. The perennial investor's problem when such a situation arrives: do you just write off your investment and put it down to experience, or do you follow the Labouchère method? When on a losing streak double up your bet? I wasn't going to put another £100,000 in, which was what they wanted. I did invest £25,000 just to protect my initial investment.

Nine months later the business went into liquidation. I had lost £125,000. It was a painful and expensive lesson, but it was a lesson well learned. Go with your instincts. Don't be greedy.

I had a lot of spare time and was thinking about starting another business, which might include some consultancy.

Whilst at MKA I had met, and become very friendly with, John Thornton. We had worked on a couple of software projects together. John had been in local government for almost all of his working life. He was in his forties. He was now managing director of a company called IPF. IPF provided IT and organisational consultancy to the public sector, especially to local authorities. IPF was a wholly owned subsidiary of CIPFA, The Chartered Institute of Public and Financial Accountants. CIPFA was the professional body for accountants working within the public sector.

Having heard that I was now available John asked me if I would be interested in joining the IPF board as a non-executive director. He wanted me to help them to grow their IT consultancy side. I was flattered, delighted, and at a loose end. I joined the board. We would meet in London once every quarter and I would be paid a fee.

It wasn't long after selling Hadley Hutt that we were approached to sell the rest of the MKA Group. Ann had been running the business in my absence.

The local government software market was becoming crowded. It was time for some consolidation. Prior to Hadley Hutt I had had discussions with regard to selling MKA or merging it with one of our competitors. The discussions never came to anything.

One of the past approaches had been with a company called MVM. MVM had developed some land charges software. Land charges deals with various items of red tape that arise during the sale and transfer of a property or land.

Since my previous discussions with MVM they had been bought by Anglian Water. Anglian Water was keen to expand the MVM business, and now approached Ann regarding the potential purchase of MKA. Ann, with the help of another shareholder, Tony McClelland, handled the whole sale on her own and in July 2000 MKA was sold to MVM. Ann would stay on with the new owners for a period of time and then leave.

I wanted to carry on doing something so I would do some business mentoring and consultancy whilst still retaining my role as a non-executive with IPF.

There are always plenty of opportunities out there. It is just a case of identifying them, seizing them and knowing what to do with them once you have them.

Luck, and being in the right place at the right time, plays a large part in one's success. So it was with Higgs and Sons. Higgs was a large firm of solicitors in the Black Country in the heart of the West Midlands. They were established in 1875 and in many ways a lot of their systems and procedures were simply a development of how "it had always been done", which in the early years had literally been pen, or even quill and paper. Today it was just a little more modern. They used computers, but not to a great extent. They didn't even have email.

Ann had used Higgs for the sale of MKA, so they knew us. They had heard that I was available and approached me to ask if I would be interested in helping them bring their IT systems up to date. It was now 2001. We had a few meetings and it was finally agreed that I would be their IT consultant working for two days per week, or as was necessary.

I now had two roles to keep me occupied: non-executive director with IPF and IT consultant for Higgs and Sons. I had stopped mentoring new start-ups. I still had spare time.

Over the years we had had a lot of work carried out on both The Summer House and Hitterhill. Some of that work was electrical.

We always used Emile for our electrical work. Emile was efficient and reliable. He was also a very keen fisherman. During one conversation with him, he told me about an idea he had that would help when setting up fishing rods in a new location. It appeared, according to Emile, that when fishing in new areas you had no idea how deep the water was, and therefore would not know what length of line and type of float to use. It was trial and error and could waste valuable fishing time. A problem if you were in a competition.

Emile's idea involved what was basically a colour-coded measuring tape. He had made a prototype, which he proudly showed me. The tape, which resembled a workman's retractable measuring tape, was about ten feet long. Emile said it could be any length. Rather than numerical measurements on the tape, it had different coloured sections. Each section was eighteen inches in length. The first section was designated "A" and coloured white, the second section was green and designated "B" and so on. The tape had a weight attached to it and it in turn was attached to the end of the rod. Once the weight was cast into the water it would unravel the tape until it rested on the water's bottom. The angler could then see which colour on the tape was at or just above the water's surface. All that was then necessary was for the angler to take a pre-prepared rig which consisted of the correct length of line, weights and float for that depth and attach it to the rod. Simple, quick and easy.

I had fished quite a lot in my youth and it seemed like a good idea to me. I had money, I had time and I knew how to start a business. After several discussions we set up Rainbow Developments, calling the product, not unreasonably, the Rainbow Fishing System. We applied for, and after several attempts, got a patent on the design and started to market it. By now I had invested several thousand pounds.

We advertised in the major fishing magazines and as a result got several orders. The problem was the cost of advertising was considerably more than the revenue it produced. We approached a number of fishing tackle shops, but they didn't think our idea was as good as we did.

Another good idea and a lot of money spent once again came to nothing. After eighteen months we gave up. Perhaps I wasn't as good as I thought I was, or perhaps I was learning lessons that I needed to learn. It was time to take stock.

COMPOSTELA

In 2000 Ann and I had taken part in an organised walk in the north of Spain. The walk was an ancient pilgrims' way dating back to the time of St James and was called the *Camino de Santiago de Compostela*. There were several starting points, but we, like so many pilgrims, only did the last 100 kilometres. The total route, starting in France, is over 790 kilometres. By walking the last 100 kilometres you could obtain a *Compostela*, which was a certificate to say that you had been on the route and completed the last 100 kilometres.

There were thirty of us in the group. We had a guide, who was also a qualified first aider and was excellent in dealing with the many blisters and falls that occurred. Our luggage was transported ahead to a prearranged night's accommodation and a meal, so we only needed light daypacks. A mini bus went ahead of us and provided lunch every day, usually in a lay-by or a quiet spot in a forest.

The *Camino* has its history in past religious pilgrimages. People do it for many reasons, not all religious. They may have or have had a serious illness. They may have recently lost a loved one, or it might just be the Everest in their life. Whilst walking you meet and greet a wide range of other pilgrims, all recognisable by their packs, Leki poles and pilgrims' shell hung around their neck or pinned to an often rain-soaked jacket.

It was a great experience and we really enjoyed it. It had given us a taste for doing the whole 790 kilometres. We spoke about it on many occasions, but there were always reasons why taking five weeks out was a big commitment. Now the businesses were sold, Emmie and James had left home and we had few commitments. Higgs and IPF could manage without me for a few weeks. In April 2003 we decided to do it.

We estimated that it would take us six weeks. We were going to walk the *Camino Français*. This route is one of the most popular. We would start in St Jean Pied de Port, which is in the French Basque country close to the Pyrenees. As the name suggests, it was the footpath gateway to the *Camino*.

Over the years the whole route has been marked out by previous pilgrims using painted yellow arrows as guiding markers. The arrows were drawn wherever the previous pilgrims had felt they were necessary. They could be on any convenient location including footpaths, walls and trees. It made the route very easy to follow.

This time we would be on our own. No support, no transport waiting for us if we wanted lunch or a lift and certainly no prearranged accommodation and evening meal. Once we had decided to do it we knew that we needed to be fit. This meant practice. We would regularly do a sixteen-mile walk with backpacks containing house bricks. This would simulate the weight we would actually be carrying on the walk. Whilst you try and keep clothing to a minimum and only pack bare essentials, nevertheless, the pack can soon become heavy, especially when you are carrying it over a long distance.

There is a very good guide to walking the *Camino*. It gives routes, potential accommodation and lots of useful tips. The only problem was that the book was heavy and carrying it in our backpacks would only add to an already heavy load, about sixteen kilograms. We did take several items of clothing that we wouldn't need, but it was too late once we had started.

Before you start the *Camino* you need to obtain a pilgrim's passport from a recognised pilgrim office. We obtained ours in St Jean Pied de Port. At each day's overnight stop the pilgrim needs to get their passport stamped with an official stamp. In this way when you arrive in Santiago de Compostela at the last pilgrim office you are awarded your *Compostela* certificate based on your stamps in your pilgrim's passport.

We left St Jean elated that we were at last doing the walk, but concerned as to what lay ahead, especially as our first walk would be over the Pyrenees; more importantly, if we would be able to do it. Our first decision came before we left St Jean. The guide book had suggested two alternative walks for the first day. One was eleven kilometres and the other was twenty-four kilometres. Out of caution, we opted for the shorter one.

The first week was very difficult and despite the fact that we had practised a lot of backpack walking prior to leaving the UK, we still got blisters.

The main thought for each day was where and what we were going to eat and where we were going to stay that evening. We did not want to put pressure on ourselves by having to achieve a certain destination each day, so the only accommodation we had booked in advance was our first night, before we started, in St Jean Pied de Port.

The terrain was very mixed. Sometimes you would be walking on roads, including at the side of motorways. Others you could be walking through forests, or over mountains, often extremely muddy. The weather was changeable and heavy rain and the mud were our constant enemy.

After the first week, with blisters healed and our feet hardened as a result of the extensive walking, we settled into a routine. I would tend to walk ahead and we would stop when we felt like it. We stayed in small guest houses. Just having to think about the walking, having no mobile phones to answer (we turned them off whilst walking) was physically tiring but mentally rejuvenating. At the same time, it was very peaceful and a way of life that I could get used to.

We usually walked at least fifteen miles every day. Once again, as we had experienced on our shorter previous walk, we encountered many other pilgrims of all ages and nationalities. They could be walking, riding on horseback or on bicycles; all accepted ways of traversing the *Camino*. We would meet and greet a pilgrim and then not see them again, or we might meet them several days later. It was rather like being in a fraternity.

One such pilgrim was an older German man whom we nicknamed Hans. He was short, about sixty years of age and was obviously an experienced walker. We had seen Hans several times. One such occasion was when we were walking through what could only be described as a mud bath. The going was very tough and Ann was struggling. I walked ahead, looking back to make sure she was all right. She also had a whistle with which she could call me if necessary. She had lost her voice several days previously through sheer exhaustion. So, the whistle was often in use. As Hans came past me he ranted in German, which I understood to be along the lines that I should not have left Ann behind, and he then disappeared over a hill.

The next time we met Hans was about one week later. He was in a cafe in a small town on the route. It was early in the morning. We had stopped to get some breakfast. Hans was no longer the sturdy walker he had been. He looked even smaller, somehow beaten. He was a broken man, in a terrible state. He was visibly frustrated, almost in tears because he could not make the waitress understand what he wanted. It was hot milk. Speaking Spanish, I ordered his hot milk and explained in German what I had done. I asked him how he felt and where the pain was. He removed his walking socks; he had already taken off his boots. His feet were bleeding and covered in blisters. Whilst we had some plasters, we did not have anything that would help Hans.

As Hans was drinking his hot milk with tears running down his face, a group of Spanish cyclists came in. They could see the poor condition Hans was in. Speaking Spanish, they asked Hans if he needed help. They didn't speak German. Switching between German and Spanish I explained the problem. With the help of the cyclists' medical kits we managed to bandage Hans' feet.

We never did find out if he completed the *Camino*, but we had experienced at first hand the spirit and camaraderie of the *Camino de Santiago de Compostela*.

There were parts of the walk that we found very hard, but the fact that we did not know what was ahead meant that we just kept going and accepted and tackled whatever challenges we met.

We would usually stop around lunchtime for a *Menu del Dia*, a concept introduced by Franco to ensure that every worker had a good lunch, at a price they could afford. We were walking in non-touristy areas so for three to five euros you could get a full three-course meal with tea or coffee, bread and, often, a full bottle of wine. Lorry drivers took full advantage of this, including the wine!

On many occasions we got so wet that our clothes would not be dry by the next morning. They soon dried out after we had been walking for a couple of hours in the sun.

The *Camino* has hostels along the route called *albergues* and are run by the Confraternity of Saint James. They provide, for a very small amount of money, a bed for the night, usually bunk-beds in a large dormitory with other pilgrims. They also provide a hot meal and showers which vary between warm and freezing, but it is first come first served and they would often be full by five o'clock in the afternoon.

By now we had been walking for nearly four weeks. Most weekends, providing we were in a town that appealed to us, we had a day's rest. Sometimes we stayed for two nights.

We were nearing the end of our walk. We had three more days to go before we reached our end goal, Santiago de Compostela. This would mean a total of fifty-three miles over the three days.

The walk so far had been physically tiring, but mentally resting and refreshing, especially after all of the recent pressure of selling the two businesses, although I had decided to look at starting another business on my return.

Whilst walking we had nothing to worry about except basic survival in terms of eating and sleeping. We had forgotten problems which, before leaving the UK, had seemed onerous and ever present. We knew they would still be there on our return, but now we could do nothing about them, so why worry?

Our normal routine, if we had one, was to look at a map in the evening, decide how we felt based on that day's walk and from that, whether to do a longer or shorter walk the next day. Having made the decision and chosen a suitable potential overnight stay for the next day, we would phone ahead and book something, always speaking Spanish out of necessity.

We decided our penultimate night would be in what appeared to be a very nice old mansion house that was not too expensive. Although we could now afford luxury hotels, we wanted to stay in basic, but comfortable, accommodation which was in the spirit of the *Camino*. The mansion house seemed to fit the bill.

Using my best Spanish, I booked a room with two single beds. We had learned that double beds on the *Camino* were generally uncomfortable, small and sagged in the middle.

We had begun the day in good spirits knowing that we were nearly there with only two more days to go. We arrived at our old mansion house at about four o'clock in the afternoon, having walked about fifteen miles. It had been difficult walking and the day had been very hot. We were ready for a drink, some food and a good night's rest.

The mansion house was an imposing three-storey building, in Georgian style. We went up the five steps to what appeared to be the front door. On the door was a handwritten note in Spanish saying that all enquiries should be made at the nearby farmhouse. We could see what appeared to be a small building about 200 metres away. Ann was worn out so she sat on the steps whilst I went to the farmhouse.

About eighteen months before going on the walk we had converted the stables at Hitterhill into a home for ourselves, keeping one and a half acres of land as a small pasture and some formal gardens. Since only Ann and I now lived in Hitterhill we rattled around the 6,000 square feet of space that it was. It seemed sensible to downsize and sell our large home. We were even considering spending more time in Spain.

Just before commencing the *Camino* walk, and with the stables now ready to move into, we had put Hitterhill on the market. We had had several offers, one of which we had accepted. It was due to complete whilst we were away.

I spoke to the lady at the farmhouse who informed me that they did not have a reservation for us, and the mansion house was closed. I knew that this was incorrect because I had spoken to someone on the telephone the day before, and confirmed that I had used the correct telephone number.

We had no option; we had to find alternative accommodation. I asked how far the nearest hotel was and she told me that it was in a town some six kilometres, about three and three-quarter miles, away. She gave me the telephone number of the hotel. We had already walked about twenty-four kilometres that day. We were both tired and needed to find somewhere overnight. There was no option but to walk the extra distance to the town.

On the way back to Ann, I turned my mobile on in order to call ahead to the hotel to ensure that they did have accommodation, which they did. After making the call my mobile rang to say I had a voicemail. It wasn't good news. I went back to Ann who was already close to tears. 'If you want to cry, now is the time to do it,' I told her. 'We have no accommodation, we have to walk another six kilometres and we need to be there by seven this evening or they will let the room go. Oh! And the house sale has just fallen through.'

It was still very hot as we set off wearily on our way. We arrived at the edge of the town about one and a half hours later. It was a large town, with a lot of traffic and people. We stopped someone and asked where the hotel was. He gave us lengthy directions which suggested that we still had some way to go; in fact, we had another three kilometres.

We arrived just before seven. They still had a room. We checked in and went straight to the bar. I am not sure that I have ever seen a gin and tonic and large beer go down so quickly. We had two days of walking to go, a total of about thirty-two miles, fifty-two kilometres.

At dinner that evening Ann said that she wanted to do the rest of the walk in one day. I thought she was joking, but she wasn't. I told her that I was happy to, but we needed to make an early start, seven o'clock in the morning, and there was to be no crying or moaning.

The next day, five weeks after starting, we arrived in Santiago de Compostela at seven thirty in the evening. We walked through cobbled streets and small, dark alleyways until we came to the large square in front of the basilica of Santiago de Compostela.

We embraced one another and cried. We were tired, but elated… we said we would do it again.

We had two more things to do before checking into our already reserved five-star Parador Hotel in the square. We had to go to the *Compostela* office to show our pilgrim's passports and to be given our

Compostellas in recognition of our journey. The office was just closing and they were amazed that we had walked so far in one day.

We also had to go into the basilica and say some thankyous. Inside there were several monks dressed in habits, each taking it in turns to pull on ropes which were attached to the *Botafumeiro*. The *Botafumeiro* is a silver-plated censer, weighing eighty kilograms and 1.6 metres high. The rope pulling causes the *Botafumeiro* to swing from side to side in front of the altar.

The *Botafumeiro* is suspended from the ceiling. It contains burning incense. It is said that apart from the religious significance of the *Botafumeiro*, swinging it has the effect of purifying the air from the pungent smell of pilgrims who have recently arrived.

We had completed our journey, but there would be many more we would complete together.

ENCRIPTION

I was being kept busy at Higgs and by 2005 we were implementing some really interesting computer technology within the business, including automatic time recording at the click of a mouse. My non-executive position with IPF became less challenging. They didn't seem to have the appetite for pushing some of the boundaries that needed pushing. I resigned.

Whilst walking the *Camino*, and having plenty of time to think, I had started to get ideas about starting yet another business. It had been in the back of my mind ever since. I wasn't sure that my success in starting and selling the previous businesses had been sheer luck or not, and reasoned, not too logically, that if I could start another successful business, then it would not just have been pure luck. I also enjoyed the challenge that a new venture gives; of course, forgetting the heartache and problems that always occur along the way.

The failure of the online employment business and the Rainbow Fishing System had certainly made me doubt myself and my judgment. I wasn't going to give up, but what to do, what business to start? That was the question.

I had been breakfast networking in the past and had not particularly enjoyed it. It is where the new ideas for business can be found, although they tend to be small. I decided to try it again.

There were a range of businesses, from companies printing business cards "better than anyone else" they said, to off-the-wall-ideas which were so badly thought through it just made me cringe.

Breakfast networking is as it sounds. You arrive at an agreed venue, normally a hotel, at seven thirty in the morning, have coffee and probably a bacon or sausage sandwich. During this time, you talk to the other people who are there, getting to know them, trying to find out what they do, judging whether you could work with them or not, and of course promoting what you do, or what you plan to do.

Each week one of the attendees gives a ten to twenty-minute pitch on their idea. At the end everyone does a round-table sixty-second pitch where they stand up and tell everyone why they are there, and what they are looking for.

When it came to my turn to give the sixty-second pitch I briefly gave my background and said I was looking to invest in, and become involved with, a new venture. I knew technology and that was where I wanted to invest, but I was open-minded.

There was nothing obvious amongst the people I had met so far, and certainly nothing of interest. Several people approached me. I think they could see a potential for easy funding. Nothing got me even slightly excited or interested until a man in his thirties called Campbell did a pitch. He was good at presenting and obviously knew what he was talking about. Campbell's pitch was that he could fix any IT problem that other people had been unable to solve. That was a brave claim.

We got talking over coffee and bacon rolls. Campbell's real expertise, however, was in IT security.

He had been in IT security for about seven years, which was a long time as IT security was almost unheard of back in 2005.

Campbell told me he had been very involved in securing the data held electronically within the British Archives' computer systems. He had also been working with the police on IT security issues, although he did not go into any detail about what exactly he had been doing. His father had been a close-protection officer in the Metropolitan Police, so I assumed there may be some sort of connection there.

The element of IT security that really intrigued me was when he told me that he was an ethical hacker, otherwise known as a penetration tester. Apparently ethical hackers hacked IT systems, using exactly the same tools and techniques as malicious or illegal hackers would. The difference was they only hacked a system with the formal consent and written permission of the organisation that had engaged them to test their IT security.

Campbell told me that usually the ethical hackers worked in black-box mode. That is, they were told nothing by the target organisation. They would therefore be in exactly the same position as a malicious hacker, who was planning an attack.

The first phase, apparently, was to carry out a *discovery exercise*. This involved searching the Internet, social media and other sources to see what information was in the public domain and therefore freely available. Apparently, the information was often very easy to find. It could be relevant to the target organisation, or indeed an individual within the organisation. The information discovered could include employees' details such as email addresses, home addresses or even payroll and bank details. Some information leaked unknowingly by an organisation's misconfigured computer systems could allow a hacker, ethical or not, to gain access to, and control of, computers, servers and mobile devices.

The hacker and ethical hacker were both looking for the same thing: information that would assist in a hacking attack.

After nearly forty years, I was very experienced in IT. I knew about malicious hacking; it was now a big problem and getting worse. I had never heard of penetration testing or ethical hacking as a defence against it. Here was my new business.

Just one small problem; I didn't know Campbell. He had been running his own security consultancy. He apparently knew several ethical hackers to whom he sub-contracted assignments that he had been given. When the work was completed Campbell would invoice the organisation who had employed him, making a margin on the difference between what he was charging the client and what he was paying the sub-contractor.

I didn't know how good he really was, how reliable he was and whether I could work with him. I needed to find out. I had a small project at Higgs that I could use him on. It wasn't security, but it was a difficult IT problem which, to date, no one had been able to solve. Campbell did. We worked well together and we got on. I had one more thing to do: market research.

I thought that penetration testing was a great idea, but I didn't know if there was a market for it, how big the market was, and how much competition there was already in the market. I soon found out.

Several reliable reports suggested that the IT security market (it was difficult to find any specific reference to penetration testing) was going to grow exponentially. I also discovered that there were not many players in the market in 2006. There appeared to be about twenty fairly large ones, but penetration testing was only one element of what they offered. Many also provided security consultancy and installed secure IT networks.

The problem I saw with this was that when carrying out penetration testing, you had to be completely objective and not make assumptions or take anything for granted; which is what they are likely to have done if they had implemented the systems. I didn't see how it was possible to provide security consultancy or install an IT network and then test your own work to make sure that it was secure. No matter how good the Chinese walls it seemed to me impossible to remain objective and to be in a position where you criticise your own security work. For this reason, I decided that we would set up a company that would only provide penetration testing/ ethical hacking services. It would not sell any related products. It would not fix any problems/vulnerabilities found, only report the problems/vulnerabilities, say what the effect of them being exploited could be and give advice on how to remediate them.

In this way we could remain completely independent and objective. I also reasoned that such independence would allow us to provide our services to consultancies who delivered security consultancy and installed IT networks, but did not have a penetration testing service of their own. This would prove to be a very good decision.

I decided to go ahead and set up a new company with both of us as shareholders. I knew that Campbell didn't have much money, if any, to put into the business, so investment was all going to be down to me.

I had enough behind me as a result of the companies we had sold. I was still working for Higgs on a part-time basis and getting fees. Having worked with Campbell for a short time it quickly became obvious that I would need to finance him whilst we built the business, especially as he would have to give up his own business to concentrate on our new venture.

I wanted to keep costs down as much as possible to start with so Campbell and I would both be home-based. In these early days we did not need the overhead of offices. Campbell was going to be full-time. With a family – he had a partner and two boys aged four and six – and a mortgage to support, he needed to be paid a regular living wage. On the other hand, I would be paid nothing and this would be the case for eighteen months.

The next thing I needed was a name for our new company, a

recognisable brand and a website. Even though the penetration market was still in its infancy, all the obvious WWWs, such as Hackers, Ethical Hackers, IT Security, were already taken. I needed a name that was easy and relevant. I came up with "Encryption", but that was not available.

Most of my good ideas have come as a blinding flash, completely out of the blue, such as leaving South Africa, and so it was with "Encription". Simply by replacing the "y" with an "i", I had a name that was available, was easy to remember and say, and was relevant to the service we were offering. We developed a logo which consisted of a thumbprint and the words "Encription Verified". The thumbprint seemed especially appropriate.

On 6 May 2006 Encription was born. Now all we needed was some business.

If I was going to sell our services I needed to get up to speed, and very quickly. I knew how IT infrastructures worked and how networks were built and functioned.

Talking to Campbell, reading a few books and spending a lot of time on the Internet soon got me up to speed.

I learned that there were two types of hacker: the ethical hacker, also known as a penetration tester or *white hat* hacker; the second was the malicious hacker, or *black hat*. Both types of hackers do the same thing, but with different objectives. They attack an individual's or an organisation's IT security. They use the same tools, techniques and approaches.

If hacking an IT system, whether it be a large network or one individual computer, they need to know which IP address or addresses to target. IP or Internet Protocol addresses are similar to telephone numbers. Once you have someone's telephone number you can call them. If they respond you can communicate with them, whether it be verbally or via electronic means, email, texting and so on. If there is no response then there is no communication.

In the same way, once a hacker has an IP address they can call it, otherwise known as *pinging* it. The hacker uses freely available software, or openware, to ping the IP address. If the IP address is live and connected to the Internet, it will echo back to the hacker's software ping. The *white hat* and the *black hat* then know they have a live target, and can communicate with it. That is, attack it.

All working elements of a computer system, even if it is a home computer, have an IP address. If there is more than one element then there will be an equivalent number of IP addresses. Other elements can include servers, desktops, laptops, printers, mobile devices and many more. Every element of a computer system is controlled and addressed using its IP address. Once a hacker has an IP address, and knows that it is live, they can launch a hacking attack on it and everything that is behind it.

The art of making IT systems secure is to make sure that only recognised and authorised users can gain access. Even when they have been given access, what they can or cannot do should be controlled by the level of privilege they are given.

An accounts assistant, for instance, may only be given access to the online accounts system. Should they try and gain access to other systems or data, to which they are not privileged, the IT infrastructure and security should reject them.

Failure to implement such controls and set up sufficient defences against unauthorised access can result in the system being hacked.

Keeping IT systems secure is a full-time job. There is no silver bullet. Having anti-virus software is only one part of implementing security measures. It is important to keep all software up to date with the latest security patches. The problem is that software updates can, in themselves, introduce new vulnerabilities.

New attacks are launched with frightening frequency. They are generally identified quickly by the anti-virus companies, and other organisations whose job it is to keep on top of such attacks and issue advice on prevention techniques. The problem arises in working out how to defend against them, and if necessary, issuing a new security patch. This can take anything from a few hours to a few days. During this time, all IT systems that could be affected by such an attack are vulnerable. These attacks are known as *Zero Day Exploits.*

If IT security is defeated by a hacker, the hacker may have full control of the IT systems and be able to do whatever they want, including changing data, stealing data or manipulating the system to do something to the hacker's advantage. It can be surprisingly easy.

It became apparent that hackers operate in anonymous communities. They learn of the existence of one another, and of each other's successful exploits and hacks through online forums. These forums are by invitation only. Once a would-be hacker is part of the inner sanctum, they have access to the dark web, where they can download new exploits and software with which to carry out a malicious attack, as well as upload their own devised attacks for others to use.

Originally hackers hacked as an intellectual challenge, a little like completing a difficult crossword. The hackers would then post in various online forums the exploits they had successfully carried out, and hence gain recognition amongst their peers.

Initially there was, in the majority of cases, no malicious intent. It was just a computer geek who wanted to push the boundaries of what could be done, sitting in their bedroom in whichever country they lived.

As an example, the geeks might set some free software they had downloaded running overnight. The software is programmed to trawl the World Wide Web identifying IP addresses that are live and connected to the Internet.

Providing a computer or IT system is switched on, its IP addresses will still be responding, or *pinging,* even if the system is not being used.

Having identified live IP addresses, the software, which has been updated with the latest known vulnerabilities, will check to see if anything behind the IP addresses is susceptible to any of those vulnerabilities.

On waking in the morning, the geek will check how many vulnerable IP addresses have been found. The geek now becomes a malicious hacker, randomly selecting which IP addresses to attack. Unless they have targeted a specific organisation, their attack will have been completely random. It could be a home computer, or it could be a major government department.

Flushed with the success of their exploits, the geeks soon become aware of the potential rewards from their actions. Not to mention the potential peer recognition. Their pursuit of pushing the boundaries of technology is replaced with the potential for financial gain.

It was not long before criminal gangs became aware of the potential that hacking offered. Why would they risk an armed robbery, the collateral damage that could result from it, and the ease with which they could be caught, when they could achieve the same thing, and possibly more, from the safety and anonymity of their own computer, possibly in a foreign country?

Governments have seen the strategic benefits of cyber-attacks on other nations. Cyber warfare is rife and has been for some time. It is just not publicised for obvious reasons.

As my research continued I became more interested in the role of, and the differences between, the malicious hacker and the ethical hacker.

The malicious hacker is carrying out an illegal act. They are accessing an IT system or computer without authority. Once the malicious hacker has breached the IT security defences, dependent upon the level of privilege they have been able to gain, the IT system is theirs to do with as they will. They can take complete control of the system: steal or destroy data; redirect transactions, including monetary ones, and other IT traffic to their own systems. In fact, with the appropriate privilege, they can do almost anything they want to do.

It will depend on the reason why they launched the attack in the first place. If the attack was launched for financial gain then they may want to redirect financial transactions to their own systems, or steal as much confidential data relevant to their objective as possible; perhaps selling it to a competitor, or holding the hacked organisation to ransom.

If the hacker's intent is just to cause disruption – they may be being paid by an organisation's competitor to do this – then they will want to cause as much damage to the IT infrastructure, website and IT systems as possible; perhaps resulting in it not functioning correctly or, in some cases, simply stopping it working.

The ethical hacker's objectives are different. Their sole purpose is to assist in making the IT security as robust and secure as possible. They are looking for vulnerabilities in the system that can be exploited.

If the ethical hacker finds that it is possible to compromise or steal anything, or indeed any other vulnerability, they make a note of how they achieved it, or could achieve it. With this information, the client, or at least their IT department, can re-create the attack and see for themselves the effect.

The ethical hacker, with the client's permission, may test their theory on a small portion of the data or system. In this way they can conclusively prove that the vulnerability can be exploited and show what the effect of it being exploited is. They then document and put forward an action or a series of actions that need to be carried out to defend against or remove the vulnerability and make the systems more secure; thus making any malicious attacks much more difficult, if not impossible, to perpetrate.

In 2006 both the good and the bad guys were still relatively inexperienced, but they would all learn very quickly.

The methods and the type of attack used by both the malicious hacker and the ethical hacker will vary according to the target, but they will both use the same basic techniques, which include, for example, finding someone's personal details via social media and using that information to make direct contact with that person. This is often achieved by the hacker pretending to be someone else who has similar interests or contacts to the target.

The different types of attacks on IT systems include an external attack, which is executed over the Internet from a remote location. The remote location could be anywhere in the world, providing they have Internet access, perhaps even from someone's bedroom.

An internal attack is carried out from within the environment where the IT systems are housed. So, the attacker does not have to defeat the external defences as they have already passed them. Internal access such as this is achieved by physically getting into the computer environment, usually by posing as someone who has authority to get such access.

Both malicious and ethical hackers can gain internal access using various means, but they nearly all involve the use of social engineering. Social engineering, in the context of information security, refers to the psychological manipulation of people in order to persuade them to perform an action, allow unauthorised access or to divulge confidential information.

A type of confidence trick for the purpose of information gathering, fraud or system access, differs from a traditional "con" in that it is often one of many steps in a more complex fraud scheme.

Social engineering often involves physically posing as someone from perhaps the organisation's IT support company, or an external contractor who needs to carry out some emergency repairs. Once inside the building it is simply a matter of finding a computer connection into the IT systems.

The damage that can be done from an internal attack can be far greater than that of an external attack. The majority of cyber-attacks are carried out by someone who has internal access to the IT systems; in many cases an employee.

The targets for both ethical and malicious hacking attacks include computer systems, mobile devices, software applications, websites and wireless routers; in fact, any element which is part of the IT infrastructure.

The advent of the Internet of Things (IoT), which connects ordinary household goods such as an oven, fridge or heating system over the Internet to a mobile device, allowing the householder, or business owner, to control the appliance remotely, opens up a whole new range of opportunities and targets to be hacked. As does the new technology now being used in cars by the automotive industry.

Given the fact that more and more national infrastructure, such as electricity and gas supplies, traffic lights, hospitals and emergency services are being controlled by computers, the threat escalates and the consequences become more serious almost by the hour.

I had decided that, for the time being, I would carry on working for Higgs. It allowed me to be flexible, still deliver a good service to them, and at least have an income stream for both Campbell and me.

My market research had revealed that none of the players already in the ethical hacking/penetration testing market were selling to SMEs, Small to Medium Enterprises. There must be a market there, I reasoned. My plan, as ever, was to deliver a quality, value-for-money service. This would surely be something the SME would understand and need.

Although I hated breakfast networking, it was an ideal way of promoting Encription and pitching to SMEs. It had also of course introduced me to Campbell. I signed up for as many breakfast networking clubs as I could, always on the understanding that they would each guarantee me a twenty-minute talking slot at at least one meeting.

My talk needed to be factual and not overt selling. It needed to explain, in plain English, what the threats were and how penetration testing could help. I had learned a lot in a very short space of time, so was able to talk knowledgably and handle any questions.

The talks seemed to go down very well. I spoke in London, Birmingham, Bristol and Bath, and after every session I had several people come up to me and ask me to come and meet them, or to give them a call. I had follow-up meetings with several of them. I was delighted. Encription was showing all the early signs of success.

The follow-ups were a different matter. It became obvious that the average SME thought that they would never be hacked; why would they, being so small, be a target? They didn't feel the need to do anything, especially when it involved money. It would usually take at least two days to carry out a penetration test and write a full report. The cost started at about £1,500.

It transpired that SMEs were totally apathetic. They couldn't see how spending £1,500 could protect them and their organisation from a potentially much greater financial loss. This was despite the fact that I had explained that because the larger organisations had, up until now, been the targets, they had taken positive actions, including having regular penetration tests undertaken, to make themselves more secure, and hence harder to hack. This meant that the hackers were now going for softer targets. The low-hanging fruit. The SME.

I had explained that hackers used software tools that they set running and left running overnight, or even for days. These tools identified computers connected to the Internet using their IP address. It could even be a computer owned by the SME I was talking to.

As a result of the output from the software tools the hackers were able to gather a great deal of information, such as what version of Microsoft was running on the computers found.

It is a fact, I explained, that everyone's Internet connection, including home ones, are scanned on average every three minutes by an unauthorised outside *agency*. That agency may be a potential hacker or software, such as Google, that crawls the web looking for information.

It made no difference. The "it won't happen to me" mentality prevailed. It would be at least another six or seven years before SMEs would wake up to the fact that they were in fact targets, and only then because they were forced to by the larger clients to whom they were suppliers. The larger clients needed proof that the IT systems of their suppliers were secure.

I needed to go back to the marketing drawing board. I analysed what I thought to be the potential markets. It was obviously the larger organisations to whom our competitors were selling. These included banks and corporates. These organisations understood the risks, had budgets to address them, and shareholders who wanted to be assured that the business' IT systems were secure.

There was, however, another market, and it was one I knew well. The local government market. Security across the whole of government had become very high profile and was being driven by GCHQ and its cyber division CESG. CESG was originally called the Communications-Electronics Security Group. It is now known as the National Cyber Security Centre or NCSC.

NCSC is the group within GCHQ which provides assistance and advice to government departments, and others, on their own communications and IT security. In doing so, NCSC set compliance standards that every government department, including local government, had to adhere to if they wanted to connect into the Public Services Network, or PSN.

The PSN is used to securely exchange information between organisations including government, police, fire and rescue, health and many others. Each organisation had to create a connection using what is known as a Code of Connection, or CoCo. The beauty of all of this was that it had been mandated by NCSC that all government IT systems that connected to the PSN must have their Code of Connection tested annually by a recognised independent penetration testing organisation who had specific qualifications. That could be us. All we needed were the qualifications, and to be on the approved list.

Obtaining the qualifications involved each penetration tester/ethical hacker sitting a recognised formal examination, which was both written and practical. There were only two schemes which ran these examinations. One was called CREST, the other the Tiger Scheme.

It had become obvious during our short time together that Campbell knew several people within the security community and they knew and respected him. He was much closer to the people in the Tiger Scheme, so we joined the Tiger bandwagon.

Campbell sat and passed the requisite examination and shortly after, Encription became a Tiger Scheme "Recognised Testing Organisation".

Because the advent and awareness of hacking was so new, there was a shortage of cyber experts and especially penetration testers to defend against it. In starting Encription I had already decided that we would employ our own staff and not use contractors, as most of our competitors did. The problem we had was when we tried to recruit experienced testers, we found that they were not, in Campbell's opinion, very good and wanted unjustifiably large salaries.

I recognised from my past experience that when you are in the services business, the assets wear the shoes, and if not treated well the assets can, and will, walk. We also had the challenge that the nature of what we did meant that it was essential that testers kept up to date with the latest attacks and undertook research and development to counteract these, so time had to be put to one side every month for a tester to do this.

The result was that we would only expect a tester to carry out revenue-earning work for 75 per cent of the available working time. The knock-on effect of this, of course, was that we could only earn 75 per cent of their full revenue-earning potential. But this would mean that we had competent, up-to-date and happier testers. At least to start with. It was easy to calculate exactly what their potential revenue-earning capability was, which was often less than some of the experienced testers were asking for.

I also believed that, being unknown, we needed to establish a customer base and hence reputation quickly. The best way of doing this was to make our day rates lower than our competitors. At least initially. Hence the reason we would not employ, indeed could not afford, experienced testers. We had to find another way of getting testers.

It was at this time that another idea occurred to me.

During the MKA era we successfully ran a training company which not only provided training for clients in the use of our software, but was also very involved in providing retraining on behalf of the government to get unemployed people back to work and young people into work for the first time. We specialised in training people in IT and as computer engineers.

I decided that over the next nine months, Encription would start a second company which would train people to be penetration testers. This would of course include our own new trainee recruits.

We would use our relationship with the Tiger Scheme to become Tiger Training Partners. With this status, we could deliver courses to individuals who wanted to learn how to be penetration testers. Because of our Tiger training we had also gained approval from NCSC to be an official examination centre where anyone, including our competitors, could send their testers to sit a NCSC recognised examination, which if they passed meant that, providing they worked for an authorised penetration testing organisation, they could security-test government and local authority systems.

Whilst it meant that we were potentially helping our competitors to recruit ready-trained testers, the income that the training generated helped our cash flow and increased profit.

The business had been slow to start, but was now performing well.

Our strategy had been to concentrate on penetration testing, and that was what we were doing. Our clients now included engineering companies, small building societies and some councils.

Being in cyber security can result in some strange requests.

And so it was in our early days. We received two different emails out of the blue. One was from a man in Australia who had obviously found us on the Internet. By now we had a website up and running. It transpired that whilst taking his finals at university a few years previously, he had suffered a family tragedy. As a result, he had not achieved the grades he needed to obtain his degree. His question was, could we hack into the university computer and change his results? He would of course pay us. The answer was of course NO.

The other email was from a private detective. It was the first, but would not be the last. The private detective had been retained in a potential divorce case. He wanted to know if we could hack into the computer and mobile phone belonging to the wife. We were to ascertain what emails and texts were being sent and received. Most of the requests from private detectives involved a wife or husband who thought that their partner was having an affair.

The rules and laws surrounding ethical hacking are quite clear. It can only be carried out with the written permission of a person or persons who have the authority to let you access the computer systems being targeted. In certain circumstances, ethical hacking can be carried out without the permission of the owner of the target where it is believed, and there is some proof, that a crime has been committed.

Furthermore, when hacking a system, it should be done to recognised standards of integrity and no data should be stolen, changed or tampered with; unless with the express permission of the person who gave authority to test the system in the first place.

There were other emails where we could help. Out of the blue we had an email from a charity that dealt with refugees, both here and overseas. The charity's website had been hacked by unknown attackers. As a result, the website was no longer accessible. The charity relied heavily on their website and had contacted other security companies like ours to see if they could fix the problem and get their website up and running.

All of the organisations the charity had contacted said that they could help. At a cost. The average quotation was £10,000 to look at and rectify the problem. Being a charity they did not have that sort of money available. We were busy, but both Campbell and I wanted to help. After some internal discussions, we agreed to do it for nothing.

We started the investigation. It didn't take us long to restore the charity's website to working order and advise the charity what additional security to put in place to ensure, as far as we could, that the same attack could not be repeated. The website was back up and running within twenty-four hours. We had one more job to do.

We now turned our attention to the attackers, which we were entitled to do as they had committed a crime by attacking and defacing a system without permission.

We quickly discovered the IP address from where the attack had taken place, which suggested that the hackers were not that sophisticated. It turned out to be a fairly simple matter to gain access to the attacker's system. Once we had access we were able to discover that the attackers were in fact a jihadist group. It appeared that they had objected to some of the things that the charity had said online in support of child refugees and their protection. The jihadist group had also been denounced by the charity.

The jihadists' attack had been in retaliation. It was clear from the data that we had been able to access on their systems that they were planning to launch other attacks shortly on other sites.

We still wanted to be within the law. The fact that a crime had been committed, and our intent was not to commit another offence but to solve an offence that had been committed, allowed us to put our plan into action.

We disabled the jihadist IT systems. For the time being anyway.

Most of our business to date had come through referrals or word-of-mouth introductions. These kept us busy as we were still a small team. I had signed up to various tender sites, especially those that were relevant to the local government market. The problem was that there was still a lack of awareness that ethical hacking/penetration testing existed, hence the number of tenders requesting quotations for such a service were few and far between.

Those tenders that did appear, we responded to. One such tender was for the provision of an annual penetration test for a council in the west of England. It would initially be for one year, but the council had an option to extend it to three years.

Tender responses are a time-consuming task. The people evaluating the tender responses want them to be presented in a methodical manner so that the answer can easily be tied back to the question. And of course the answer has to be relevant, preferably adding value for money. Not properly answering the questions which are being asked by the tenderer will almost certainly result in rejection.

I spent many days, and nights, on this response, ensuring that we answered the questions in the order they were being asked and correctly, as well as suggesting other approaches to their security. It was to be a two-stage process.

Stage one was submission of the written response. If that was successful, the tenderer would be shortlisted and asked to attend a round-table question and answer session.

We submitted our response and waited anxiously for the result. Two weeks later we were informed that we had been added to the shortlist of three companies. As a result we were invited to stage two, a round-table meeting at the council offices.

There were ten people from the council ranging from IT to procurement and legal. The questioning was thorough and detailed. I felt that we had responded well and fully to the many "what if?" questions we were thrown. We now had to wait to see if we had been successful.

The letter arrived one week later. We were the successful bidder. We had won a one-year contract. It was worth over £11,000 per year. And there was the option to extend it by a further two years.

The payment terms had been agreed as quarterly in advance. When the first cheque arrived we photocopied it and framed it. Both Campbell and I felt that this was the start of something big. But was it?

At the start of 2007 we had been trading for nine months. We had carried out several penetration tests for a variety of clients. The workload was increasing. It was time to consider finding some offices.

Working from home had worked well initially, but we needed a base and somewhere where we could work together and talk face to face on a daily basis.

A recent incident had made the need for proper offices even more urgent.

In addition to the tender we had recently won I had been having discussions with another local council. I had been dealing with the head of IT. We had got on well together. As a result, we now had a purchase order for several security tests which we were to undertake for them over the next six months. The purchase order was addressed to our registered office which was Campbell's home address, a terraced house on the edge of Worcester.

Shortly after we received the purchase order I had a call from the head of IT who said he was very sorry but he could not deal with us, and was withdrawing the purchase order.

It transpired that one of his people had driven past our "Registered Office" and seen that it was in fact a privately owned terraced house. We were devastated, but I was not about to give up that easily. I explained why this was the case, in that we were a recent start-up, which he was aware of. I asked him to give us thirty minutes with his technical team to prove our capabilities, and to show that where and what our offices were was largely irrelevant. He reluctantly agreed. At the meeting with the technical team, Campbell was brilliant. The council's IT team were clearly impressed. Our purchase order was reinstated and they became a long-term client.

We needed offices that we could bring clients to if necessary. They had to have car parking and they must be able to provide a comfortable and good working environment. They should also be in easy travelling distance for both Campbell and me. After visiting many options, we finally found some on the edge of Worcester. They were old stables, but had been sympathetically converted into offices. They were in a quiet, rural setting and had car parking. We moved in four weeks after we had found them.

Due to our growth we were now at the stage where we needed to consider recruiting additional resource.

Ann was a trustee of a local hospice. As a result of this Ann became friendly with the lady who ran the hospice's charity shops; her name was Alison. One day Alison was talking to Ann and happened to mention that her seventeen-year-old son had just been suspended from school, for hacking the school's computer systems.

As soon as I heard this I asked Ann to get Alison's son to contact me. In ethical hacking it is very rare that anyone who has carried out illegal hacking will be employed by a penetration testing company, for several reasons. The first is that they are unlikely to get security clearance, which is necessary. Secondly, there is a concern that once they have tasted the illegal side of hacking and its potential rewards, it can be difficult not to be tempted to go to the dark side again.

After meeting Alison's son, he had convinced me that he had just been trying to see if he could do it, a little like the early hackers. He had succeeded. He was very keen to learn and had a good personality. James H became our first employee and for me set the standard of the sort of employees we would recruit going forward, preferably without them having tried illegal hacking.

James H was not interested in going on to university, but he obviously had a natural bent for computers and, specifically, hacking. Because of my background I had developed a passion for developing people, based not on their academic qualifications necessarily, but on their enthusiasm and how much they wanted a job. Going forward I would interview many university graduates who, quite frankly, were useless. Even though many of them had studied computer science at university, the depth of their cyber knowledge was often, to say the least, superficial. Their grasp of the English language and ability to write a concise and meaningful report was even more dire.

I would often set them a written English and grammar test at the interview. My favourite was to ask them to explain in writing the rule of offside in football or leg before wicket in cricket. Several failed based not on explaining the rule, but on their grammar and spelling.

For some reason we never got female applicants, otherwise I would have had to change the subject.

I believed then, and believe even more now, that there is no shortage of potential candidates who could become penetration testers, both male and female. They are probably in mundane jobs, on the dole or just wasting their lives playing computer games in their bedrooms. Many of them have an innate talent that they are unaware of. A talent that remains untapped.

THE NEXT MOVE

By 2009 we needed to consider moving premises. The Stables had been good for us; it had been a great working environment and had been cost effective. I always prepared quite detailed business plans which allowed me to keep track of our performance and growth, as well as our cash flow. The business plan was never a target that I was bound by, but it did give me a guide as to when we needed to take corrective action, including cutting our costs, and when we should go for more growth.

My business plan suggested that if we could maintain our rate of growth (we had had a revenue at the end of our first year of £33,000 and by the end of year two this had risen to £160,000), with the necessary increase in personnel to cater for our predicted growth, we would need about 2,500 square feet of office space. This would allow for growth over the next five years. A big jump from 600 square feet, which the Stables had been.

We didn't want to move from Worcester, but every office I looked at, the rent was too expensive for the amount of space we needed. The minimum started at about £40,000 per year, £16 per square foot, plus about £25,000 per year for rates. There was also a lack of car parking. So I was forced to look further afield.

Near to where I lived there was a modern industrial estate. It was in Kidderminster. The units had always caught my eye when I had driven past. They were known as The Towers. They were very modern looking. Made from aluminium. I knew that some of them were empty. I discovered that the rent was only £5 per square foot, approximately one third of the cost in Worcester and the rates would be £4,000 pounds per year. The unit we were considering had ten car parking spaces.

We signed a contract on the unit. It had 5,000 square feet of open space. I was thinking big, and it was going to cost me less than half of the amount the new space in Worcester would have cost. Encription House in Foley Park, Kidderminster was born.

All of the units on the estate were industrial units, designed for that purpose, not for offices. This would mean converting the majority of the space into offices. Which would be expensive. Encription House was a shell. There were toilets – one male, one female – and a small kitchen. Partial central heating had been installed. There was a second floor which was reached via an internal open metal staircase. The staircase resembled a wide fire escape.

The mezzanine floor, which it led to, only covered two thirds of the downstairs area. It had metal railings where it abruptly ended apparently in mid-air. On the ground floor there was a drive-in bay obviously meant for deliveries. There was an electric roller door which gave access to the bay. The upstairs mezzanine overlooked this bay, obviously designed to make sure that vehicles coming and going could be watched from above, and providing more height for the larger vehicles. My eventual plan was to make use of the bay area for another purpose.

We had to get quotes to line all of the walls as they were still the bare skins showing metal struts that the builders had left. After all, they were industrial units. We initially wanted to create at least three ground-floor offices. It had also become obvious that during the summer it would get very hot and that we would need to install air conditioning. This was all going to cost a lot of money, £60,000 to be precise. It was £60,000 we didn't have.

We had been banking with NatWest Bank for three years and had always kept within our overdraft. To my mind we had been ideal clients, doing what we said we would when we said we would. We approached them. Our bank manager at the time was always eager to help and he suggested taking a loan through a government-sponsored loan guarantee scheme. The bank would lend us the £60,000, but if we went bankrupt then the government would meet 90 per cent of the outstanding balance. The loan would be repaid over five years at an agreed interest rate. Two years later NatWest would not be so helpful when we needed a short-term increase in our facility.

We were still growing and still looking for staff. By now scheduling the work and the testers was becoming almost a full-time job, so I decided to advertise for someone. The interviews all took place upstairs on the mezzanine floor with nothing but a small desk and two chairs on a bare concrete floor. There was no point in hiding the fact that we were small, but growing fast.

I had interviewed several people, but none was what I was looking for. Then Kate came in. She was very bubbly and really wanted the job. She didn't have any experience in IT, but I felt that she could be trained, she would fit in and I could work with her. I offered her the job and it proved to be one of the best decisions I ever made.

As a result of the increased workload we continued to recruit. One such recruit was Umer. Umer was from Pakistan and had a computing degree from a second-tier London university. He lived in London, so we agreed to interview him at Paddington Station which, he said, was convenient for him. Umer was about twenty-three, very well groomed. He dressed smartly, in what looked like an expensive suit with a white shirt and a red tie.

The interview went well. He had a pleasant character. We thought he would be good in front of clients. His IT knowledge was quite good, but we would have work to do to get him up to our standard. We thought six to nine months. After some discussion, we decided to offer him a job.

We always took and followed up references, both personal and technical. Umer said that he could not give us any references in the UK. All of Umer's references were in Pakistan, but he had lost touch with them. This should have rung alarm bells with us, but for some reason it didn't. We were desperate for more resource. We hoped that we wouldn't regret it.

We told him that he would need to move to Worcester. Many future recruits who were geographically remote from our offices would be allowed to work from home. This would also give us countrywide sub-offices. But in Umer's case we knew we would need to spend a lot of time training him. Once he was ready we would consider letting him return to London.

Umer knew that he would be paid a very low starting wage until he had proved himself. In the majority of cases, the low starting wage was not a problem for the new recruits as they were desperate to be given a chance to get into ethical hacking, and Encription was one of the few companies taking the risk at this level. From our perspective, the fact that they were prepared to take a low wage showed us that they really wanted the job and were willing to make sacrifices to be given the chance and get trained. It also gave both of us time to see if they were going to make the grade. Once trained their salaries would increase rapidly.

Umer never really made the grade and seemed to be absent on several occasions, making various excuses for his non-attendance.

I arrived into the office early one morning; once again, no sign of Umer. I had already decided that he needed to go. Around ten o'clock Umer called to say he had family problems and would be in sometime later. At eleven o'clock we had a visit from the police who asked us several questions about Umer.

Three months later he was sentenced to six years in prison for indecent assault. The local newspaper reported that he had been found guilty on two counts of rape and six of indecent exposure. Not to mention being under the influence of drugs. He had apparently exposed himself early in the morning in the centre of Worcester whilst saying 'I am a hacker, who wants to fuck me?'

We didn't make any more mistakes like that.

In the years to come I would employ gas fitters, electricians and adolescent geeks. It was the bored teenagers who were driving their parents mad by locking themselves away and spending all of their time on a computer, occasionally coming out for meals, that I was looking for.

Once we started advertising we were inundated with applications. We wasted a lot of time interviewing candidates who obviously didn't have a clue, let alone any meaningful IT knowledge. Our solution was to create an online test.

Candidates had twenty minutes to complete the test and were given three lives. Using a life would give them an additional clue, but would count against them in our assessment of their capabilities. The objective of the test was to first of all discover where in a computer system, which we had set up, the password was. The problem was that once they had found the password it was encrypted and they had to decipher it. The test proved to be a valuable tool in screening candidates and eventually we would not interview anyone unless they had successfully passed the test.

Martin had passed the test. He said that he found it easy. He had not had to use any lives. Martin lived in Worcester and had apparently not particularly enjoyed school. He did not want to continue in education. He was seventeen. He decided, or more probably his parents decided, that he should pursue an IT apprenticeship. IT apprenticeships were a relatively new innovation in 2009.

We had been sent Martin's CV by the apprenticeship organisation to which he had applied. As well as teaching the apprentices about IT, the organisation was also required to find them relevant work placements.

Martin would work for us for a fixed period. We would pay him the minimum wage, £3.68 per hour. He would go to college one day per week and every three months he would be away from us for training with the apprenticeship company. This would last for two to three weeks. Martin would learn more about information technology. The apprenticeship was one year.

It was obvious that Martin had a lot of talent for IT, but he was very shy, perhaps as a result of all of the time he spent in his bedroom on his computer. Martin had only been with us for four weeks, but we could see his potential, and didn't want to lose him to someone else. We decided to offer him a job as an apprentice penetration tester.

Whilst with us it became obvious that he was indeed very good at IT and took to ethical hacking as though he had been doing it all of his life; perhaps he had and just not told us!

His experience with what he was being taught by the apprenticeship company was entirely different. It became obvious to us, and to Martin, that he knew more than the lecturers.

This is one of the problems with IT education. Anyone who is any good can earn a lot of money "doing IT". They do not earn nearly as much teaching it. Whilst there are exceptions, in the main the quality of person teaching IT is not as good as it needs to be. We pulled Martin off the scheme. Today Martin is earning a very high salary and drives a new BMW.

Another trainee recruit was Anthony. He was also very shy. Shyness seemed to be an inherent trait of most IT geeks. Anthony was a qualified electrician who lived in Leeds and was desperate to get into IT security. Like Martin, he was self-taught. He had passed our online aptitude test and we invited him for interview.

We could see Anthony's lack of communication through shyness being a problem in client situations. It was only when he told us that he kept snakes and had devised a system that allowed him to feed them remotely, adjusting what and how much they were fed using his mobile phone, that he became enthusiastic and animated. We offered him a job.

Martin and Anthony were typical of our recruits. Some did not work out and we had to part company with them, but our success rate in identifying potential talent was high. Our need to find new testers and keep the existing ones happy became even more of a challenge.

New recruits usually took three to six months to train. That was three to six months of pure cost and no revenue. We never put anyone on revenue-earning work until both they and we were happy that they were ready and would do a good job. Once they were ready, or *cooked*, as I would often describe it, it created a new challenge. Recruitment companies. Every tester was contacted at least once per week by a headhunter offering greener fields and more money elsewhere. We lost very few in this way, but it was a distraction we could do without.

As a result, I decided to recruit an HR manager. Initially the post would be part-time. Dawn had considerable human resources experience with some very large companies. She was used to travelling all over the country and working very long hours to deal with staff issues. She now had two small children so wanted to spend more time with them. So, the offer of a position that was part-time and close to where she lived suited her very well.

I had been unsure whether an HR manager, even part-time, would have enough to do. I needn't have worried. It didn't take

Dawn long to introduce formal appraisals and find new avenues for recruitment.

One such avenue was the forces. Dawn discovered that there was a formal channel through which you could advertise vacancies that men and women leaving the army, navy and air force had access to.

We had several applications, mostly of a very high standard and often from candidates who had been in the special forces. These were potential candidates who were used to working behind enemy lines in Iraq and Afghanistan. They knew how to carry out covert surveillance and were very technical and computer literate. What is more, they were used to working long hours away from home or base.

If we had one complaint from our existing testers it was that they were often away from home too much, despite the fact that we only expected 75 per cent utilisation from them. The problem was that we were so busy that they often had to work at 100 per cent-plus utilisation.

The recruitment of ex-special forces personnel would make our approach to IT security, and especially social engineering, much more innovative and sophisticated.

CHECK STATUS

In 2007 we were looking to become a CHECK company. CHECK companies are examined and approved by NCSC, the National Cyber Security Centre part of GCHQ. Only CHECK companies and suitable qualified employees of those CHECK companies can carry out security testing on government systems that handle and process confidential data rated above a certain security level. Most government systems hold such data.

The security of data is measured in Impact Levels or IL, starting at zero and going up to six. As its name suggests, the rating is a measure of what the threat, or impact, would be to security if such data were stolen or compromised. Information that is already in the public domain, such as that you would read in a daily newspaper, is rated Impact Level zero. Names and addresses held as data, depending on what they are used for, would probably be rated Impact Level one. If the national insurance numbers of those people were held in a separate file that could not be connected with the correct name and address, that would also be Impact Level one. Once the two files can be matched so that it is possible to ascertain a person's national insurance number, name and address then the Impact Level increases probably to two. Impact Levels of four and above are designated top secret. The higher the number, the more sensitive the data is.

The criteria for becoming a CHECK company is very stringent and in two stages.

The first stage is that the company must submit sufficient proof that it is financially viable, is already delivering penetration testing services to an acceptable standard, and that the testing reports the company produces after each test are sufficiently detailed and explicit. This means that the report shows that the correct in-depth testing was carried out, which was relevant to the target(s). The evaluation also ensures that the remediation advice given in the report regarding what actions need to be taken to remove or reduce the risk is specific and relevant.

If the company satisfies all of these criteria, then, after more background checks, it is declared a CHECK Red Light Company. This means that the company has satisfied the first part of the accreditation towards CHECK status, but is not allowed to undertake testing for government bodies under the CHECK scheme until it is declared Green Light.

To achieve Green Light status, the Red Light CHECK company must employ at least one certified CHECK team leader. That is someone who has passed a recognised NCSC examination. The CHECK team leader must have lived in the UK for at least the last five years. They must hold a full UK passport and be able to pass detailed security vetting.

There are two recognised levels of CHECK tester: team member and team leader. The difference is that the team leader has to be able to show substantial practical penetration testing experience over a period of time. At least three years. They must also pass a much harder two-day examination consisting of both written and practical testing elements.

The CHECK team member must also sit an examination, which is still very hard. The examination lasts one day. CHECK team members only need twelve months past practical and demonstrable experience. All CHECK team members, regardless of level, must resit their examinations every three years.

There are only about sixty CHECK Green Light companies. All are UK-based. It is very easy to lose Green Light status if you do not maintain the high standards required. Every CHECK test that is undertaken once you are a CHECK company has to be submitted to NCSC to make sure that it meets the standards. Once a penetration testing company has CHECK Green Light, it opens up a whole new market, which is only available to CHECK companies.

I decided to apply for CHECK status in June 2007. It took me at least three days to gather the necessary evidence and complete all of the paperwork for the first part of the application which would give us Red Light status.

Two months later our application was rejected. NCSC felt that our reporting was not up to the standards required.

Once rejected you cannot reapply for twelve months. We reapplied again in 2008. We had made our reports clearer and much more comprehensive. It had been a good lesson for us. This time we got Red Light status. We were ecstatic because we knew it would mean a lot more business, and that business would be with the government.

Campbell had already sat and passed the requisite CHECK team leader examination and had more than three years' demonstrable experience. In November 2008 we gained CHECK Green Light status.

As a CHECK Green Light company, your company's details, and those of your approved testers, appear on the GCHQ-NCSC website. It is to this website that government bodies go to select an approved organisation to carry out penetration testing at the highest levels of security. Because the entry requirements are so difficult there are usually no more than sixty companies on the list.

Getting CHECK status changed the whole momentum of the company. Organisations were now contacting us and asking us to quote or tender for business. As at the start of Encription, I continued selling and looked after everything commercial including legals, accounts and cash. Campbell and his ever-growing team did the testing.

Our clients became many and varied. They included many corporates both small and large, airports, councils, fire and rescue and health services and, of course, government departments. Much of the work that we undertook was classified.

It was whilst testing one quasi government organisation that Campbell discovered a website which he thought should not be there. The website was running on a very secure, and critical, part of the IT infrastructure. He of course brought this to the attention of the security manager.

When a security weakness is discovered during testing it is rated as low, medium, high or critical. Critical generally means that it is possible to change important parts of the system, or indeed take complete control of the system. If a critical vulnerability is found it is standard practice to stop testing immediately and to inform a designated point of contact, usually the person responsible for security: the information security officer or ISO.

Having informed the organisation's information security manager, who was unaware that this website existed on the system, he asked Campbell to investigate further. This would mean that Campbell would have to undertake a digital forensic investigation.

As an example, when people delete files on a computer they assume that the data has been deleted. In fact, it is only the index which says where the data is on the computer that is deleted; the data still exists. The analogy is a filing cabinet containing many different files where the location of each file (which drawer it is in, what title it is held under) is recorded and accessed by using a paper index at the front of the filing cabinet detailing what file is held in which location of the filing cabinet; thus, enabling someone to find the file and its contents simply by looking at the index. Remove the paper index entry for that file and it becomes much more difficult, if not impossible, to locate the information, but the files and their data are still there. Only the index has been removed.

The same principle is true of computer-held data and files.

It was obvious that whomever had put the website on the IT network had tried to cover up their actions by deleting files and information they thought might lead to them. Using standard computer forensic techniques and tools we were able to recover the files, see what actions had been taken, from which terminal and when, making it possible to trace exactly who had created the website and when.

The website was in fact managing the membership and accounts of a local golf club. It had been created, and run, by three employees in the IT department. From the information we had gathered we were able to recover a series of deleted emails which had been sent between the three and the golf club. The emails described how the site would work. Some emails contained detailed confidential financial information of the golf club.

Having obtained and documented sufficient evidence with which the culprits could be confronted, we presented it to the information security manager. The evidence had been gathered and documented according to the Association of Chief Police Officers (ACPO) guidelines. So, if necessary, this evidence could be used at a tribunal or in a court of law. It didn't go that far. The three employees were disciplined and dismissed.

To me this was obviously a new business opportunity. There were several organisations offering standard forensics for crime-scene investigations. There were also forensic accountants who were able to investigate financial transactions that had been part of a fraud or similar crime. There were very few organisations offering computer forensics. There appeared to be a large untapped market.

Three months later Encription had a new forensics division. I also had a use for the bay in Encription House. It would become a digital forensics laboratory.

Our techniques for both penetration testing and social engineering had become much more sophisticated. As was our approach to conducting a security exercise in general.

Usually a client would approach us and ask us to test a particular network or element of their IT systems. This is fine for certain purposes, including identifying what security vulnerabilities exist at that point in time. But it is rather like drawing up a balance sheet for an organisation showing their assets and liabilities at that exact moment. If the organisation then purchases a new asset or disposes of one then the balance sheet changes.

So it is with penetration testing. A new vulnerability could be introduced to the system the day, or even the hour, after it was tested. It is for this reason that regular automated vulnerability scanning needs to be undertaken on a regular basis between penetration tests. Vulnerability scanning uses software that is updated with the latest known vulnerabilities. It highlights any new vulnerabilities in the system under test.

Because of the human element in penetration testing, penetration testing is much more thorough, and consequently takes more time and costs more.

The other problem is that penetration testing does not take into account the human element in security. It is nearly always the human factor that compromises IT security, whether that is clicking on an unknown website, opening an unsolicited email, or unwittingly divulging confidential information.

Our service was to become more comprehensive. We would still do penetration tests, but now many of our exercises would be spread over three to six months, or even longer in some cases. During this time, we would use social engineering techniques to engage with employees and try and elicit confidential information from them. We would try and gain unauthorised access to buildings and IT systems and we would introduce daily vulnerability scanning of computer systems to ensure that the latest attacks were detected and stopped.

We had been working with a large European IT company who provided security consultancy and services, but not penetration testing. They had a well-known client who was launching a new multifunctional website aimed at teenagers. The site allowed the teenagers to play a selection of games, try their hand at quizzes, enter competitions and buy merchandise. Success in a game or quiz would result in prizes.

The client wanted to outsource the development, running and support of the website. The website would be developed by the European consultancy with whom we were working. It would be hosted and run on another third party's computers. Ongoing technical support would be provided by yet another third party.

Our brief was to not only test the security and resilience of the website and the IT systems on which it was to run, but also to test how secure the third parties were and if they or their employees could be compromised or persuaded to divulge confidential information regarding our mutual client and their website. We told them that it would be at least a three-month exercise.

Our first target was the website, which was not yet live. It was still in the testing stage. It didn't take us long to find several vulnerabilities, including being able to load a malicious program by entering it in an area that was reserved for comments from users.

If there is an area on a website into which an address or a comment can be input, under certain circumstances that same area can be used by the hacker to type in a program, unless the web developer has ensured that only alphabetic characters and numbers are allowed to be entered. Programs need to use special characters such as = and * in order for them to work. If the web developer has allowed these characters to be entered, simply by not checking for their presence, the hacker is able to load a program into the area. The program will then be executed by the computer hosting the website with potentially disastrous consequences.

The malicious program entered may be designed to encrypt or wipe all of the data held by the computer. Encrypting the data could then result in a ransomware attack, where the data will remain encrypted until a financial ransom is paid to the attackers.

Once we had entered our malicious program into the comments area and it had been accepted by the website, it began running. Its purpose was to encrypt all of the data. It was a ransomware attack.

We had reported our initial findings and the vulnerabilities had been fixed. We now turned our attention to the various games that were available. Once again, we found that by writing a fairly simple program and letting it play the games as though it were a human, we could win every time. Had this been on a live system it could have been very costly, not only financially, but reputationally.

After extensive testing, and remediation, we were satisfied that the website was secure and ready to go live.

We now turned our attention to the third parties whose computers were running the website and whose people were providing support to website users. As part of the exercise we had been able, via various techniques, including social media, to compile full background details on the key IT and management personnel within the supplier's organisation. We knew their family backgrounds, their home telephone numbers and, in several cases, their log-in credentials with which they accessed their organisation's IT systems and data.

Getting confidential information from individuals can be very easy or it may be extremely difficult, according to how security-aware the target is. Using social engineering we called several third-party suppliers' support staff who were looking after the website and its IT infrastructure. We also contacted those answering users' questions and providing software and hardware fixes where necessary.

The straightforward social engineering approach is to call the support desk and pretend to be someone else. In one case, we said we were a member of the IT department of the owner of the website.

Our story varied depending on what information we were looking for. We said that we needed to integrate elements of the website into some of our own systems, and in order to do this we needed the third-party support staff to set us up as a website user but with full administration rights. This meant that once we logged into the website with these user privileges we could do anything we wanted, including bringing the site down.

We said that we would, for security purposes, send them an email confirming our request. All we had to do was to set up a new email account and simply transpose two letters in the email address, or make a minor change to it. So *edward.jones@xyz.com* could become *edward.j0nes@xyz.com*, changing the alphabetic "o" for a zero. People are not trained to look for such things, and very often do not look at the sending email address, so they are easy to exploit. The same technique could be used with a website address taking the unsuspecting person to a website that was identical to the one they knew, but was in fact a copy. Any payments made would go into the criminal's account and no goods would be delivered.

After receiving our email we were given administration rights to the website. We could now do whatever we wanted to do with it. We simply reported what we had achieved.

Getting email addresses within an organisation can also be a simple matter. All you need to know is what sort of person's address you want. Someone in accounts, IT, personnel, the choice is yours. The ethical hacker, and the malicious hacker, would telephone the organisation and ask for that person's email address, on the pretext that they had been asked to send that person some information, an invoice or perhaps a CV. Once in possession of the email address, the hacker can send an email purporting to be from a genuine person who has a legitimate reason to email. Simply responding to the email or a read receipt request can provide the hacker with valuable information. If the unsuspecting recipient replies, the email response may contain valuable information about the IT network from which the reply was sent.

Out-of-office receipts can also be invaluable for social engineering exercises. They tell you exactly how long the person is going to be out of the office for; an ideal opportunity to visit the organisation when they are away on the pretext that you have an appointment with them. Once in the building it can be easy to carry out covert surveillance, gain entry or ask pertinent questions that will aid the attack.

The level of expertise and attention applied to ensuring that communications are handled correctly and securely will make the hacker's job easier or not. The information, unwittingly divulged, due to lack of IT security training, expertise, or just poor configuration of the IT systems, may include such details as what versions of operating system are in use. With this information the hacker will know what vulnerabilities exist in that version of the operating system. They could then use that knowledge to launch an attack that makes use of that vulnerability.

If the social engineering approach is carried out with sufficient confidence and authority, then it is generally successful. People innately like to be helpful, and when they believe that the request is coming from someone with authority, especially if that someone is a client, or at least they believe they are, then they will do their utmost to be helpful.

Using the direct approach in this case yielded a great deal of information which we could use later in an attack, but more importantly it showed us that the third-party support staff needed security awareness training and they needed it quickly.

We wanted to test the security of all aspects of the third-party support function that we thought could have weaknesses. This included the reception desk in the various suppliers' offices. It wasn't difficult to obtain a copy of each of the suppliers' logos. With these logos, and again hiding behind a cover story, we approached a small company who produced USB sticks with personalised logos. Our cover story was that we had been retained by the third-party supplier companies to come up with ideas for promotional gifts that they could give to their clients. We asked the promotional gift company if they could produce two USBs with the two logos on them. If our clients liked them then there could be a large order of 2,000 or more. The promotional gift company was more than happy to help.

Now in possession of the two USB sticks with their distinctive logos, we loaded each USB with software that once loaded into a USB slot on a computer would run malicious software, also known as malware. The malware would be undetectable by anti-virus software, as it was a new type of attack. The malware would create a back door for us via the Internet. It gave us direct access into the third party's IT systems whenever we wanted it. Once we had this access we effectively had complete control of their whole IT infrastructure.

We used the same approach with each third-party supplier. We found out where their head offices were and we went to each of their reception desks. In all cases we used both a male and a female member of our staff. They were both well dressed, which we knew would help with their credibility. In the first attack, the story was that the USB had been found outside on the pavement. In the second case, that it had been found *on a train*.

The girl with the USB found on the train said she lived nearby.

She said she knew the company as she walked past the office every day. Thought it might be important and so had brought it in. The receptionists at all locations were most grateful.

Later that day we had back-door access to most suppliers' IT systems. At a later debrief session we discovered that in one case, the receptionist herself had put the USB into her computer to see what it contained.

We had taken the precaution of loading some dummy files onto the USBs, marking the files as confidential so that, at first glance, the contents would seem important and merit passing on. Another receptionist had passed the USB onto her manager and he had loaded it.

The front-line targets for social engineering attacks tend to be those people who answer the telephones or are the first point of contact for general enquiries, be they via email or other means. In most cases these people have not been trained to be security-aware. As a result, they often unwittingly divulge confidential information, or even provide unauthorised access to IT systems. They are usually middle to lower tier members of staff. But that is not always the case. It can be those in much higher positions who are the weakest point where IT security is concerned.

In our initial investigations of who was doing and saying what on social media, we discovered that a senior director in one of the support companies was fanatical about Audi TT cars. We had found out that in fact he owned two.

We saw this as a great opportunity.

Writing a software program that if it were loaded would, once again, give us direct access and possibly control over all of the supplier's IT systems, proved to be an easy matter. Once finished and tested, the program was burned onto a DVD. The DVD needed to look genuine and exclusive. We designed a very colourful label for the DVD with a picture of a futuristic-looking Audi TT on it.

Underneath was a strapline that suggested that the DVD contained details of a new Audi which was about to be released. This was supported by an official-looking "Audi" letter saying that as an Audi TT enthusiast and owner, the director had been selected for a pre-release video tour. He would also be given priority if he booked a test drive.

Making sure that the packaging of the DVD looked equally impressive, we sent it by recorded delivery.

The DVD was loaded and opened on the day of delivery. The program was designed to send us a message as soon as it was active; within one hour of receiving the message, we had access to all of the director's emails and confidential files. Thirty minutes later we had complete remote control of all of the IT infrastructure involved in running our client's website.

The vulnerability that allowed unauthorised data and programs to be loaded was soon fixed.

After three months of extensive penetration testing and social engineering, with all vulnerabilities being fixed, the website went live to great acclaim. Our client knew that their website was secure and that the organisations supporting it were also, now, much more secure and security-aware. For the time being, anyway.

Encription's reputation was growing fast. Many potential clients were now approaching us as a result of a recommendation. By 2012 we had a wide range of clients.

The majority were still in government and public sector, but we began to win more commercial business.

We were now getting telephone calls which typically went, "We supply goods to XYZ"; usually a very large organisation. "They have told us that we need to show them that our IT systems are secure. Apparently, we need a penetration test, but we don't have a clue what that is! XYZ has recommended you."

This was both flattering and inevitable. The larger organisations had introduced security measures, including penetration testing. But they still had a few Achilles' heels, a major one being their suppliers, often SMEs, with whom they exchanged electronic data, or who had, for logistical purposes, been given direct connections into the larger organisation's IT systems.

This, and the fact that hardly a day went by now when there was not a report of some major organisation being hacked, often as a result of one of their suppliers using an insecure IT system to communicate with their IT systems.

SMEs were being forced to wake up to cyber threats and do something about it, or lose the valuable supply contracts they had.

This new awakening led to some interesting exercises. One company we had been speaking to was a small credit-card processor. They handled the processing and payment of specific store cards.

The managing director's brief was that they wanted us to look at how secure their organisation and their IT systems were. Our first approach was checking the security of their organisation. To do this we would use exactly the same techniques as a hacker or fraudster would. The first port of call was information that was in the public domain. This could be old newspaper articles, Internet postings and of course, social media, which included Facebook.

It had been a simple matter for us to obtain a complete list of all their management team, including their IT manager.

From this we found posts that he had made on Facebook. Following all of the posts and threads can be arduous, but very rewarding, and so it proved in this case. We were able to find his address, what car he drove, how many children he had (there were two and they were five and seven), what his hobbies were, and where and when he was going on holiday. It is exactly for this reason that I never used social media. A lot of people may think that such information is innocuous and of no harm or use, but in the wrong hands it can be invaluable.

This man was head of IT for an organisation that handled secure financial information. He would know all of the passwords and methods to access the IT systems, especially the financial ones. The one option that fraudsters could use, although extreme, is the kidnapping threat. It would not be a big step to find out where his children went to school and when.

The other option is to, once again, use social engineering. Social engineering has many guises from putting on overalls and pretending to be from the company's electricity or telecommunications provider, or a similar organisation, to simply being confident and walking past security and reception, then tailgating existing staff, as though you were one of them, as they walk through secure doors.

It is amazing, providing you show sufficient confidence, how easy this can be. The person you are tailgating will often hold the security door open for you.

In this way, it is possible to get access to the building and hopefully the IT systems. When a hacker has that access it is usually easy to gain access into the systems. One reason being that once you are inside an organisation you are often behind their firewalls which defend against external hacking attacks. And that is one fewer defence that you have to breach.

The method we used with the IT manager was to start chatting to him via Facebook. Our pretext was that we were also in IT and worked for a small financial institution; we had set up a dummy company just in case he did a check.

There is virtually no training in IT security awareness carried out by organisations, especially where it is most needed, at the grassroots level; the receptionist, the clerk, the shop-floor worker. Most people do not recognise a social engineering attack, and that includes a lot of IT people.

So it was with the IT manager. Once we had exchanged various personal, fictitious, details about ourselves and our company we were able to start discussing IT matters. We needed to be kindred spirits. If he supported Manchester United... so did we. If he liked a particular car... so did we. Anything that would encourage him to keep in touch.

What we really wanted to know was what his IT set-up looked like and what defences he had in place against hacking. He wasn't going to tell us this because we asked; we had to create trust.

We did this by appealing to his ego. We said that we knew that we needed to strengthen our own IT security, but were new into the job. We didn't really know how to go about it and what to put in place. But we told him it seemed as though he obviously did. Flattery works wonders.

He was very forthcoming and helpful. He told us exactly what his security consisted of. It had taken us about three weeks to get to this stage, but was well worth it.

With the information provided we could easily check if the versions of software and hardware he was using had any security vulnerabilities, which of course they did. He wasn't that good. It didn't take us long to exploit these vulnerabilities and twenty-four hours after we had been given what we needed we had access to all of their client data, both personal and financial.

We could steal the data, introduce new users, change settings and divert financial transactions to our own bank accounts. All of this was achieved from our offices in Worcestershire, but could have easily been achieved from anywhere in the world. All without having ever actually spoken directly to or met each other.

We did not, of course, steal or change anything. We had been retained to find out if their organisation and IT systems were vulnerable, and if so, to then tell them how to fix the vulnerabilities and become more secure. Which we did. Our job was done, for this year, anyway.

Getting more clients and becoming more sophisticated in our

approach meant more recruitment, more fitting out of the offices and more administration and sales staff. In previous businesses I had started, our strength had always been accounts and knowing where we were financially. It was time to recruit an accountant. After several interviews I offered the job to Mark; he was a disaster and lasted only three weeks. Then we got Victoria and she was very reliable. One thing I had learned along the way was that if you make a mistake, especially in the people you recruit, identify it and admit it early. Then do something about it. Quickly. This may mean more training or mentoring, or it may mean dismissal. I honestly believe that in everyone's interest, especially existing staff, it is better to make a decision, even if it is a hard one, than to make no decision at all.

We were also continuing to recruit additional trainee testers. Penetration testing companies were considered large if they had six testers or more. We now had twelve and were still growing.

FAMILY

By this time Emmie had completed a degree at Oxford and was married. James had also finished university.

James and Emmie both seemed fine. I loved them dearly and did everything I could to help them get on. At times I think I got too involved to the point of interference, but that was me; the control freak.

Emmie had decided to pursue a career in teaching and had initially really enjoyed it, but after four years she wanted a change.

The training side of Encription was going well and we were running regular courses in penetration testing. They were lucrative. Our success had shown us that there was a market. I had been considering recruiting a training manager for some time. Emmie fitted the bill. She knew how to teach and she was good at IT. I was, however, hesitant about bringing a family member into the business, especially my daughter. It could be difficult for her with other employees and it would certainly be difficult for the both us if it didn't work out. I decided to go ahead and take a chance.

Apart from a few early confrontations it worked very well. She would later change to sales and made great inroads into developing our commercial market. She proved to be an invaluable member of staff.

After his degree James had decided to go into the pub trade. Ever since he was a teenager he had wanted to have, and run, a nightclub, but his first career step towards this was to join the fast-track management scheme with Bass. He soon found himself managing pubs in London, where he eventually decided to stay. Like father, like son. James wanted to start his own business. His first gastro pub was in Highgate in London. This was followed by two more, also in London.

James knew how hard running a pub was so he knew what to expect. What he hadn't bargained for was the cost of getting a pub up and running, and more importantly how long it can take to make it profitable.

Disillusioned, he sold the gastro pubs and went into high-end catering. Again, starting from scratch, and with two partners, he set up kitchens on an industrial estate in Park Royal, London. The kitchens were big enough to cater for large events and the food they produced appealed to a discerning clientele. He was soon supplying some of the large companies at London Fashion Week, as well as other well-known organisations, many of them on a daily basis.

Whilst the catering business was doing well, James had had some conflicts with one of his business partners. We discussed his options, one of which was to work for Encription. I needed someone with good business acumen to support me in the business. We decided he would initially work part-time for me whilst still being involved for the majority of his time in the catering business. Twelve months later he joined Encription full-time having sold his shares in the catering business to his partners.

I was still concerned about having my children in the business, not because they weren't capable, but because of the potential jealousy that could be engendered amongst existing and new staff. I shouldn't have worried. They were both able to command respect because quite simply they were very good at what they did.

Having sold Hadley Hutt and MKA, we now had some money in the bank.

Mike, who had worked for Kwikform and had helped me on my return from South Africa, and I had grown very close to one another. We regularly met socially. Ann and Mike's wife, Sandra, were best friends, as were all of our children. They were all of a similar age. Our families almost became as one. We went on holiday to Spain several times with them.

As a result of these trips and the good times we had had, Ann and I had spoken frequently about buying a holiday home in Spain. In 1999 we decided to go out for a week and have a serious look. A local estate agent took us around. He showed us properties in the hills, on estates and in remote locations, but nothing particularly caught our eye, until he showed us a new development near Estepona called Cabo Bermejo.

We fell in love with it. Because building had only recently commenced, and we were some of the first people to view the estate, we had the choice of almost any apartment on the development. Only a show house had so far been built.

We needed to think about it. We would have to take a mortgage, but finance had already been arranged by the builder. Over a few drinks that evening we decided that we would go ahead. We particularly wanted a large terrace and we had to have a sea view. A two-bedroom ground-floor apartment next door to the show house and overlooking the beach and the sea was exactly what we were looking for. Gibraltar and the coast of Africa were directly in front of us.

We moved in in 2000 and would have many happy years there.

IRELAND

I t was whilst I was at Cabo Bermejo for a short break that I
had met Paddy. Paddy also had an apartment there. He lived
in southern Ireland. Paddy came from a family who had been
one of the largest bottlers of soft drinks and Guinness in Ireland. At
a young age he had become managing director. The business was
eventually sold and Paddy was now developing golf courses along
with big-name golfers.

Paddy and I had met through our families at the communal
swimming pool. We also went out to dinner together on a few
occasions. We got on very well.

I had been thinking of expansion for Encription for some time.
In fact, through the UK Board of Trade I had made contact with
the British Embassy in Poland who would arrange meetings with
potential partners in Poland. It came to nothing.

Southern Ireland was a different matter. It was much closer
and we had a common language; well, almost. Having found out as
much about Paddy's expertise and his background as I could over a
few drinks, I asked Paddy if he was interested in getting involved as

a business partner. It was obvious that Paddy knew virtually nothing about IT, but it transpired that he had some very good contacts who could be useful. When I asked Paddy who he knew in health in Ireland, his response was "the minister". That would be a start.

Encription in the UK was thriving and had now been trading successfully for five years. It was time to expand. We decided to go ahead and start a separate company in Ireland, Encription Ireland Limited. It was 2011.

I had already carried out a lot of market research. It was obvious that there was virtually no awareness in Ireland of the need for IT security. There were certainly no compliance requirements within government departments, as there were in the UK. In fact, I estimated that they were five to six years behind the UK in terms of IT security legislation. The competition was small in number, but large in who they were: PWC and Deloitte.

The first two years were very slow. In anticipation of getting business we had taken on a trainee penetration tester who was a recent graduate. We brought him over to the UK for three months to be trained. He turned out to be very good, but because of the lack of work he became bored and left us. We still had confidence and carried on trying to sell our services. Any business we got would be serviced from the UK.

Hacking in Ireland, as with most countries, was becoming more prevalent and certainly being reported more. One of the prime targets was the credit unions. Credit unions are banks which are established in a community and run by the community for the community. The board of the credit union could literally consist of the butcher, the baker and the candlestick maker, but it worked.

Seeing them as an obvious target both for a cyber-attack and our services, we made several presentations to credit union boards across the country, much as I had done to networking groups in the early days of Encription UK.

The responses were similar to those I had received when I did the early presentations to breakfast networking meetings in the UK. There was a lot of interest and "come and see me", "send me a quotation", but little business came out of it. Once again, "it won't happen to us" was the mindset.

The credit unions were overseen by, and responsible to, the Central Bank of Ireland. The Central Bank realised that there was a security issue. So much so that in 2013 the Central Bank mandated that every credit union must have a penetration test at least once per year.

At last we started to get substantial business. We soon had a large proportion of the Irish credit unions using our services. The tide had turned. We were also responding to, and winning, tenders for some major Irish Government bodies. Encription Ireland was becoming established and known.

This resulted in more recruitment. Despite our successes we still needed more sales. Two sales people were recruited. All the business we had won had been undertaken by testers from the UK, but with travel and accommodation, this was costly. It was time, once again, to recruit two Ireland-based trainee penetration testers. Any excess work that they could not cope with would still be handled using UK testers.

Our model in Ireland was the same as it had been in the UK. We restricted the services we offered to penetration testing, training and forensics; training and forensics being satisfied from UK resource.

We were approached by a large, well-known accountancy and audit practice in Dublin, who could see an opportunity for marketing our type of services. They were heavily involved in companies that had gone into administration and, in many cases, were the administrator. Some of the administrations had been brought about by fraud within the business. We soon found ourselves carrying out digital forensics investigations in several businesses.

It is essential in a forensics investigation to capture as much data, both live and historical, as possible. As soon as possible. Every hard drive, computer memory, laptop or computer, has to be imaged. All actions taken need to be well documented, and standard procedures need to be followed when imaging.

Imaging is literally copying the data binary digit by binary digit so that it is a true and accurate reflection of the data which was on the IT systems at the time of and during the fraud, if there had been one. This is because it may, and often does, provide evidence with regard to the crime or fraud that has allegedly been committed. It is also essential to maintain a written audit trail from the start to the end of the investigation, including when the image was taken and by whom, who has handled the imaged data and where it is, or was sent to, at any point in time. This can be a very time-consuming process, but is only the beginning of the real work: the investigation.

On one occasion we were asked to investigate a suspected fraud which involved the alleged avoidance of duty on agriculture fuel. Given that Ireland is very much an agriculture country, such a fraud is not unusual.

In this case we had recovered over one million emails from an IT system. We now needed to examine them all for emails that might be relevant to the suspected fraud. Many were emails that the owner, and in this case, the suspected fraudster, had deleted in the belief that they were deleted and therefore the evidence was destroyed.

Our accountancy partner was also the administrator. They asked us to find any email that had certain key words in it. Those key words included surnames and references to specific addresses. Using some proprietary forensic software and other techniques, we were able to recover the deleted emails and identify several which contained the key words.

From this it was possible to put together a chain of evidence that showed when the fraud had first commenced and who had been involved in it, the key dates on which emails had been sent describing how the fraud was to be executed, and by whom. We were also able to find out who had received or been sent any of the relevant emails.

We knew that there was every possibility that this case would go to court if sufficient evidence could be found. It was therefore essential that in gathering the information we followed very rigid guidelines on how it was collected, analysed and kept. If these guidelines were not followed, then the evidence could be inadmissible in court. There was also a possibility that we, as Encription Ireland, would have to appear in court as expert witnesses.

The case did go to court. We did not have to act as expert witnesses, but the evidence from our forensic investigation was crucial in obtaining a conviction. Two men went to prison for several years.

Encription Ireland had been set up as a prototype that, if it worked, could be duplicated elsewhere, perhaps as a franchise model. I would travel over at least once a month. Looking back that was not enough. Like any business, it needed more hands-on from me, especially with the lack of technical knowledge that Paddy had. I knew there was great potential there and it was only when I paid more attention to selling, and especially responding to some government tenders, that we really established ourselves.

I knew from past experience that tenders were very time-consuming and it was important, as we had done in the past, that they were responded to in the order that the questions had been asked. By following these simple rules, and paying a great deal of attention to our response so that it matched what the prospect was looking for, we won two large public-sector contracts which were each to last for three years. This changed both the nature and the profile of Encription Ireland.

A lot of lessons had been learned in setting up and running a geographically remote business, and a lot of mistakes had been made. I knew that going forward, financial control and a lot of hands-on involvement were the key.

INNOVATION

The hackers and fraudsters, who understood the potential of hacking, were becoming more and more innovative and sophisticated in their attacks. We needed to keep up with them. If not be ahead of them. The knowledge and experience that our recently recruited special forces' guys brought with them would be a major factor in the way we approached hacking and the prevention of it. These new and innovative approaches would greatly contribute to how successful we were.

The lady mayoress looked very elegant in the half-page photograph which appeared on the front page of the local newspaper. Her regalia hung proudly around her neck together with her photographic identity card. This picture would prove to be invaluable in our execution of a security exercise which we had been asked to undertake on an annual basis by the council the lady mayoress represented.

John D had been a marine for nine years. He now worked for us. He was very experienced at covert operations, mostly behind enemy lines. He was also very technical. A good programmer. He had, after training, proved to be very adept as a penetration tester.

Our objective was not only to carry out a formal penetration test; we also needed to see how secure the council offices were, and how easy, or hard, it would be to gain unauthorised access to both the offices and their IT systems.

John D was able to enlarge the lady mayoress' photograph, and in so doing get much more detail from her identity card, which was also a security pass. The pass included her photograph. When enlarged we could read all of the wording on it, including the pass number and expiry date.

Using the same font and layout as that on the mayoress' card, John D was able to produce his own identity card, complete with his photograph and security number on it. Stage one complete.

Stage two involved using Google Maps to ascertain the layout of the council's campus. In this way, we could identify the entrances and exits to offices, and any other useful information, so that we would not appear lost once we got on site. Whilst Google Maps can be used for mundane purposes such as seeing what type of house someone lives in or how to get to somewhere, in the wrong hands it can be used for very different reasons. Google Maps will show you an aerial view of Buckingham Palace, identifying all of the skylights and possible ingress points.

Stage three was physical reconnaissance of the campus. John D had made several visits to the campus, and at different times. It appeared that a good time to visit would be eleven o'clock in the morning. This was a coffee break time and when several employees went outside for a smoke.

It was a Monday. John D could see that several members of staff, as expected, were gathered outside a fire exit, where they were allowed to smoke. Casually joining the group, and making sure that his security pass was in full view, John D asked one of them for a light. John D didn't smoke… but when duty calls…

He soon got talking to the obliging employee; a man in his

thirties who was wearing jeans and a Superdry top. John D's cover story was that he was a new employee. He had only started that day so was still learning the ropes. He needed to establish his credentials and in doing so gain access to the building. The fact that he was a new boy would excuse him for any obvious mistakes he made.

When his new-found friend extinguished his cigarette, and headed back through the fire door and into the building, John D followed him. The new friend scanned his security pass and was given access to the building. John D very quickly did the same, knowing that his would not work. He had not been able to see the rear of the mayoress' card, which he guessed would have had a magnetic security stripe on it.

The new-found friend saw that John D was having problems. John D said that he had only just been issued with the card, which to an extent was true. He said that this was the first time he had tried it. If you can show that you need help then most people are sympathetic and provide that help. New-found friend was no exception. He passed his own security card to John D and John D was in.

John D wandered the building unchallenged for the next three hours. He sat at an empty terminal in a small office that had been left switched on. The previous person had logged out. Using his recently acquired hacking skills, John D soon had access to the system. He quickly found where the vulnerabilities were and how to exploit them. There was a large amount of both personal and financial information. He downloaded extracts from the discovered data to a USB he had brought with him.

By any measure the exercise had been a success, certainly from our point of view.

But John D had one last thing to do. During his time wandering the building he had noticed a laptop which was unattended. He went back to make sure that it was still unattended. The laptop was connected to a network port, so it was fairly certain that it contained credentials that would give access to the council's network both internally, and more importantly, we hoped, externally. John D simply unplugged the laptop, put it under his arm and left the building using the fire exit through which he had gained access in the first place. We could now carry out more ethical hacking from the comfort of our own offices.

Gaining access to buildings unchallenged is an essential part of testing an organisation's security. It is mostly achieved with bravado and confidence.

As a growing business we needed to be proactive in finding potential clients. It was because of this that, armed with a laptop and the appropriate software downloaded from the Internet, I would regularly tour large industrial estates. The software I had was capable of picking up wireless signals and details of their security from base stations within a building. It was these base stations that provided Wi-Fi connections throughout the building. The fact that the signal can be detected from locations exterior to the organisation means that it is possible to connect to the wireless base station whilst, for instance, sitting in a car. Which was me. As long as I only observed the signal and whether it was secured or not, I was not breaking any laws. Gaining access through the wireless connection without permission is illegal.

Once a connection is made to the wireless base station it may be possible to read and intercept all messages and data which are being sent wirelessly. It may also be possible to gain access to the IT systems.

Wireless base stations can be secured to prevent unauthorised access; so that even if the signal can be detected, access cannot be gained unless the person has the password, or other appropriate credentials. To secure a wireless base station is a very simple matter. But not everyone does it.

On every industrial estate I visited, at least 50 per cent of all wireless stations were unprotected.

Writing to the companies afterwards and telling them what we had found and how we could help should have yielded a positive response and action. It didn't. It was obvious that amongst the smaller companies, and in some cases, very large, well-known companies, apathy still reigned.

Encription was now getting regular enquiries to undertake penetration testing. But we knew from experience that whilst testing the IT systems and their elements was an essential part of security, it was only one element.

People were the other weakness in the system. We decided to introduce *Red Teaming.*

Red Teaming is similar to reconnaissance, as many of our special forces' recruits knew. Whereas a penetration test takes place over a number of contiguous days, a *Red Teaming* exercise would take place over several weeks or even months. During this period, as we had done with the multifunctional website aimed at teenagers, we would gather as much information about the organisation and its employees as we could. Depending on our brief and using the gathered information we would craft appropriate attacks. The attacks could be phishing exercises, face-to-face encounters or making contact over the Internet and using social media, and even some new ones which we would design according to the need and our objectives. We always need to be like the hackers: innovative.

We had proposed a *Red Teaming* exercise to a high-profile high-street outlet. They had accepted our proposal. We were to test the security of their head office and its staff. We had already undertaken penetration testing for them and found several vulnerabilities, some rated as critical. It was obvious that IT security was not their top priority.

During the day the head office was a busy, bustling building. It had six floors and accommodated a few hundred employees. There was a steady stream of visitors to the ground-floor reception. It proved easy to mingle amongst them. Having tried to gain access to restricted areas proved fruitless. It was fairly secure, but there were holes.

If we were ever caught, which we were on a few occasions during other exercises, it would simply be a matter of producing a signed letter which we had been given, usually by the managing director of the organisation. The letter explained the exercise that we were undertaking and why. There were, however, times when even the executive management, including the managing director, were not aware of what we were doing. In most exercises, such as this, it is essential that as few people as possible are aware that it is taking place.

Having had little success in gaining access during the day, we decided to return late at night with a team of two. From reconnaissance earlier that day, and Google Maps, we knew the layout of the building and the fact that there was a keypad on a side door. The side door should give us access to most parts of the building. It is good security practice to change the code on a regular basis, but most organisations don't bother. This keypad was no exception. When we dusted it with talcum powder, the keys that were used more than others, and were the code, were clearly visible. The talcum powder did not stick to those keys as well as it did to the unused keys. It was simply a matter of finding the correct combination, which took six tries. With good security the keypad should have disabled itself after three failed attempts. It didn't.

Once inside we were able to freely explore the building until we came to one part that was patrolled by a security guard. We had our cover story ready. It wasn't long before we met him. We told him that we were part of the computer department and were working through the night to carry out a software upgrade. We explained that it was work that could not be carried out during working hours. He accepted our story and carried on with his patrol.

Whilst touring the building we had come across a conference

room, which had CCTV cameras installed. We guessed that this room and the cameras were used for conference calls, which would probably be, at times, confidential. It didn't take us long to hack into them and create a *back door* through which we would stream conference calls, or CCTV broadcasts, to one of our laptops; thus allowing us to be party to any video conferencing without the other participants realising we were able to hear and see all of the discussions, both confidential and non-confidential, which were taking place.

It proved to be a very fruitful night, but I wondered if we had gone too far when our guys took photographs of themselves sitting in the managing director's chair with their feet on his desk.

Another successful exercise, which had been all too easy.

The testers would take maximum advantage of their five days per month in which to keep themselves up-to-date and carry out research and development. We would sometimes ask them to look at a particular area of research and development, but we gave them the freedom to explore their own ideas.

Giving them such freedom had yielded many fruitful innovations in the past, but one of the most fruitful and useful was the "Cloner". It had been John D's idea, but several testers had worked on it with him. The end product was a complex collection of microchips all sitting on the same plastic base, *motherboard,* and connected by small wires, a little like the plugboards of the ICT 558 I worked on in my early career, but much smaller and far more integrated.

The Cloner was designed to be carried in a briefcase so that it was out of sight and inconspicuous. The Cloner, once activated by the touch of a button, collected data as it was transmitted between two devices.

The data we were interested in collecting was that between a security card or security fob and the security card reader, which would in most cases be attached to a wall and gave access to a secure area. Providing the reader recognised that the encrypted signal from the card or fob was legitimate, the security gates or doors would open, and the person allowed to walk through.

When the Cloner, concealed in its briefcase, was activated, it would copy the stream of encrypted data being sent from card to reader. This data was stored on the Cloner which would allow us to duplicate it at a later date, and store it onto our own security card, thus giving us access through the security system at another time. We didn't even have to decrypt the signal.

Although we never tried it, we could see no reason why our Cloner could not have been adapted to collect secure data passed between a credit card and credit card terminal when a contactless payment was made. It is for this reason that none of us in Encription ever trusted or used contactless payments.

The Cloner became an invaluable tool in many future exercises.

There were many new innovations that came as a result of allowing the testers research and development time, and the freedom to come up with their own ideas; including a small program which took about thirty minutes to write.

The program would be downloaded if a link we had created in an email was clicked. The link could look like an email or a website address, and seem legitimate.

We also used more sophisticated methods, including hiding the download link in a logo within an email. Again, once the email was opened the program loaded itself from the logo onto the recipient's computer. It then, without them realising it, activated both the camera and microphone on the computer. This allowed us to see and hear everything the user of the infected computer was doing or discussing. Later versions of this program included a key logger, which sent every key depression made back to our host computer, where another program collected the string of characters entered and made sense of them. As an example, if the name of a website had been typed it would begin with "www". If it were a financial institution, including a bank, we could be fairly sure that the next entries would be a user name and password.

These innovations were both duplicating what the hackers were doing and helping us to be one step ahead of what they were doing, allowing us to see the full potential effects of such attacks, but more importantly to create defences against them.

The work that was coming in now was very varied and interesting. We often worked alongside the police or in some cases we were retained by solicitors and barristers.

One such case referred by a barrister was a small law firm. Although some of their clients were self-financing, the majority of their work was for clients who were eligible for, and used, legal aid.

In order to carry out legal aid work the law firm needed a legal aid operating certificate. The certificate had to be renewed every year. Without this certificate, the law firm could not undertake legal aid work. Legal aid work represented 80 per cent of their business. The firm had been in existence for several years, were well respected and, of course, renewed their certificate annually. They were therefore very confused, not to say worried, when they received a letter from legal aid saying that their certificate would not be renewed.

Upon investigation, it transpired that whoever had filled out the legal aid licence renewal form had ticked a box to say that they did not have permanent offices. Permanent offices are a prerequisite for a law firm to carry out legal aid work.

By now their licence had expired and their business was potentially at an end. They had consulted a barrister whom they knew. The barrister in turn asked us if we could help, as they knew that the form for renewal had been sent electronically from the law firm's computer systems. They suspected that someone may have hacked the system. Perhaps a disgruntled client.

We started our investigation and discovered that the form had indeed been submitted using the law firm's computer systems, but it had originated from an IP address which did not belong to the firm.

We quickly discovered that the IP address was being hosted by one of the major Internet service providers. We knew that a direct approach from us to the Internet provider to divulge who was using the IP address would not work. Under their rules of confidentiality such information will only be provided as a result of a direct request from the police, or as a result of a High Court order to divulge.

The law firm's barrister secured a high court hearing before a judge within forty-eight hours. The barrister needed to show that there was good reason to divulge this information. It seemed obvious that an illegal action had taken place, so there was good reason. The hearing lasted less than an hour and a court order for the Internet company to divulge the name and full details of the user of the IP address was given.

It transpired that it was an ex-employee who had left the law firm on very bad terms. The firm had failed to delete the ex-employee's login credentials and therefore access to the law firm's computer systems.

By examining the computer logs we were able to prove that it was this ex-employee who had made the changes to the form. We now had documented evidence showing what files had been accessed and what data had been changed. In this case, that they did not have an office. The ex-employee was taken to court by the police and found guilty. The law firm's legal aid licence was re-instated.

The majority of all computer fraud is committed by someone on the inside.

We began to get enquiries from organisations overseas and carried out several projects abroad. All of our testers were now CHECK-certified through NCSC and GCHQ. This meant that they were also security-cleared. The security clearances that the testers had meant that there were restrictions on where they could work geographically, and for whom. Several countries and governments were blacklisted. It was therefore essential in certain cases to obtain written permission from the NCSC to undertake such work. Even going on holiday to certain countries needed to be declared if a tester was to retain their security clearance. Failure to do so could result in a tester's security clearance being withdrawn. They would then have to reapply, which could take six months or more. During this time, the tester would be severely limited as to which projects they could work on.

There are several levels of security clearance. The minimum level that we applied for was SC, or Security Cleared. The person applying for the clearance, and their sponsor, in this case Encription, had to complete a lengthy form. Additionally, the applicant needed to provide a full CV going back to when, and where, they were born. There can be no unexplained breaks in their background. If they were unemployed for a time this needed to be declared, as did what they were doing during this time. References for work, academic achievements and personal background needed to be provided. Additionally, personal references were necessary. The references were contacted, and sometimes even visited and interviewed.

The next level of security clearance was DV, or Detailed Vetting. Whilst SC allows a person to work in an environment, and have access to information and data that is up to and including Impact Level four, Secret, DV gives clearance up to and including Impact Level six, Top Secret. Detailed Vetting involved more initial forms than SC, but also required a separate day of face-to-face interviews with an appointed vetting officer.

In all cases of security clearance, the purpose is to ascertain if there is anything in a person's background, or currently, with which they could be compromised or blackmailed.

Clearances need to be renewed every three years. Some applications were unsuccessful, often due to a parent's or relation's background. One of our testers was rejected because his father had belonged to a banned organisation whilst at university.

I went through and passed DV clearance, as did most of our testers.

THE BOARD

B y 2014 we were recognised as one of the major players offering a penetration testing and *Red Teaming* service. We had a seven-figure turnover and were producing a healthy profit. Because of the way that we looked after our finances, cash was never an issue.

Our major issue was people. Our recruitment policy was still the same. Take trainees, almost regardless of what they were doing now, and, providing they knew their IT and could program, train them. Dawn, our HR manager, changed the way that we recruited and handled staff issues. For the better.

One of the issues we had with some new recruits was that once they were trained, they would often think they were now rock stars. They were working too hard… they didn't want to travel and stay away as much as they did… they were having to get up too early in the morning… they were coming home too late… we weren't paying them enough. They could get more working for other penetration testing companies.

This was despite the fact that we had a policy that no tester would work more than fifteen days per month on fee-paying work, the fact that we had financed them for six to nine months whilst we trained them and had given them skills that made them far more marketable.

There were always some who wanted more, had no loyalty and moved purely for money, thinking the grass would be greener. It never turned out that way. It would not be unusual that having left, they found that they were working even harder and longer. They would often ask if they could have their job back.

It was these people, and their attitude, that would make me take a momentous decision regarding the future.

The rich pool of talent in ex-forces personnel that Dawn had discovered had mostly worked in the marines or special forces in Afghanistan and Iraq, their speciality being security, including communications interception. They had no qualms about staying away for periods at a time, generally were not money-motivated, were dedicated and just wanted to do a good job. All we had to do was train them to be penetration testers, work to our high standards and use all of the hacking tools that existed as well as those we had developed. They were also encouraged to develop new hacking tools and methodologies of their own.

Campbell had been asked to talk at a major European security conference which was an accolade for both Campbell and Encription. I was regularly contacted by the media and asked for my comments on the latest cyber-attack. We were now high profile in the IT security market. We had grown almost exponentially. But we had decisions to make about the future.

Up until now we had run the company in much the same way as we had run MKA; as a family business. It was, however, obvious that if we were going to carry on growing as we had, initially at more than 100 per cent per year, and latterly 50 per cent per year, we needed to be far more structured and to delegate responsibilities. I needed to relinquish some control and get wider views and inputs other than my own. We needed a board.

I wanted the board to be relatively informal, but to be focussed. It would meet once per month off-site. This was important because I did not want too many prying eyes and listening ears back in the office. Obviously, Campbell needed to be part of it and by this time James was working for me full-time, so I brought him on to the board as well.

I was worried that Emmie would feel pushed out, but I honestly didn't think it was something she would want to do, or indeed had time for.

I also felt that we needed some external influence on the board. Someone who was not involved on a day-to-day basis, could be objective and had the background to give sensible input. It didn't take me long to think of Steve. Steve and I had worked together back in the late seventies. He had worked for my old friend Mike as a programmer analyst, but had moved on to much bigger and greater things; first as a senior consultant with Price Waterhouse Coopers, PWC, and then as a partner at Deloitte, where he had been very successful. Steve was now semi-retired, so had time, and the expertise I needed. I approached him. He was willing and delighted.

We hired a room at a local hotel, set an agenda, which consisted of an update as to how we were trading, including financials, plus any other matters that needed discussing or action. This forum proved very useful.

The business was continuing to grow and we were continuing to recruit, which was still causing its own headaches. I had realised many years previously that I was good at identifying an opportunity, analysing it, and developing it to a certain stage. I was also good at selling. I could keep a tight rein on the financials. I was perhaps over-cautious in spending money, which restricted the rate at which we would grow, but would ensure that we remained solvent and in business.

Whilst my master plan was to be a large multi-million-pound company, I was not the person to take it there. I could, as I had done previously, put the building blocks in place, but when it came to taking on board outside investors and having to answer to them, being target-driven, I was not interested. I needed to be in control.

It was for this reason that I put an item on the board agenda which was about me. Over the next eighteen months, I would be stepping back. I did not plan to retire, as I was still passionate about what we did and the people we employed, at least the loyal ones. We now had forty-five employees spread all over the country, with another six in Ireland.

At the end of the board meeting we had put some actions into place. We would become more structured as a company. Up until now we had been a very flat hierarchy. We decided that we needed to regionalise the business and appoint regional managers, who would be selected from our testers through formal application and interview.

The challenge we had was that they were techies and had had little, if any, exposure to running a business. Which is effectively what they would be doing. It was agreed that I would do some training sessions with them. This training would include financial management and budgeting. We also decided that we would put other formal structures in place so that we could support our targeted growth. On a day-to-day basis, James would take over from me and I would effectively become chairman.

We did discuss selling the business, but we all agreed it was too soon. I had had a few approaches in the past. Some from large players. I had rejected all of them on the basis that they were not offering enough money, and I could not see how, given the profile of those organisations who had approached me, it would benefit Encription, or its people.

THE FUTURE

When we had first started training our own people how to be penetration testers, Campbell had devised an appropriate course and delivered it. He was excellent at presenting. His course was the one that became recognised by GCHQ NCSC as an acceptable introduction to CHECK team membership.

The course was four days and was a mixture of "chalk and talk" with a lot of practical exercises in ethical hacking. On the fifth day, the students took a formal examination set by the Tiger Scheme and approved by GCHQ's NCSC. The examination consisted of a one-hour multi-choice examination, a one-hour written examination and a two-hour practical examination. We would send the completed examination papers to the University of South Wales, who would mark them and communicate the results back to us, Tiger, NCSC and the students. Passing the examination, providing it had been invigilated by an independent, approved, external examiner, and had been marked and verified by an independent and approved body, the University of South Wales gave the student a formal qualification which was recognised by GCHQ NCSC as a prerequisite for CHECK membership.

It was obvious that the course was another potential income stream, so we started marketing it externally with a great deal of success. The course was always busy and many of those whom Campbell taught worked for large companies, several being competitors as well as clients. Sometimes they would become friends as well as ex-students and we would keep in touch with them; this connection often resulted in more testing business for Encription. I estimated that each course, on average, would generate up to £10,000 worth of new testing business.

One ex-student, and now a good friend of Campbell's, was Adam. Adam worked for BlackBerry. He had kept in touch. He was a regular visitor to Encription House. Adam obviously had a lot of respect for both Campbell and Encription as he would often be asking for advice with regard to security, and specifically penetration testing.

It was early June 2015. Campbell told me that Adam had been in touch with him to say that BlackBerry were planning to diversify. They would, of course, still keep their mobile phone business, but were going to set up a new cyber security division.

BlackBerry had always been recognised for security. Their mobile phones were the only ones that were security-approved by both the UK and US Governments. In fact, President Obama was often seen using one in public. Adam had told Campbell that BlackBerry were interested in buying Encription. I took it with a pinch of salt. I ignored it.

The board had laid out their master plan, which was targeting a £5 million turnover within three years, producing a very healthy profit at the same time. We were all excited by the prospect. Our plans of achieving it were in place, and I was relishing being part of it. BlackBerry's approach was a distraction, and, I still felt, not serious. Although no details had been discussed, only intents, it was becoming obvious that they were serious and weren't going to go away just yet. We had to consider all of our options. This included selling.

Adam was based in Liverpool. Things had progressed. We had exchanged non-disclosure agreements, so we were able to answer their initial questions, and to be fairly open with them.

Adam asked Campbell and me to join him and one of his colleagues for lunch in Liverpool. They took us to a very nice twenty-fourth-floor restaurant overlooking the city centre. The conversation was relaxed, and the drink freely flowing. Adam confirmed that BlackBerry were serious in looking at buying Encription. They wanted to proceed to due diligence, to ensure that everything was in order. I thought it was; that there were no skeletons in the cupboard.

Over lunch Adam asked how much we wanted for Encription. Campbell instinctively left this to me. It was a question we had anticipated and discussed.

We gave them a figure, which did not elicit any real reaction. We finished the meal with coffee and brandies. Campbell and I caught the train back to Worcester. We had a lot to discuss. This was getting real.

It had been a week since our lunch in Liverpool. We had provided BlackBerry with a reasonable amount of information, including financials. They now wanted to schedule a conference call with some senior BlackBerry people. The problem was that Ann and I were booked to go on a cruise the week they wanted the call. We would be away for two weeks and I would effectively be out of touch. The call was going to be very sensitive and confidential. It was not one that could, or should, be made over an open telephone line.

I knew that on the day they wanted the call we would be anchored off the Amalfi Coast. I spoke to the purser and explained, with a little padding around it, that I needed to make a secure ship-to-shore telephone call. He arranged it.

The call lasted for thirty-five minutes. At the end of it I was in shock. BlackBerry had made a verbal offer subject to due diligence.

It was more than we had expected, or discussed. It deserved serious consideration.

Did I need the money? By now Ann and I were financially secure. As a result of the sale of the previous companies, we had not had a mortgage for fifteen years. We were able to afford, some would say, a luxurious lifestyle. I would say it meant I did not have to worry too much about money.

Campbell was a different matter. He was keen to sell.

Asset-wise, I had already achieved my financial ambitions, at least on paper. Which of course included Encription.

There were other considerations. What about Emmie and James? I knew that, if it went ahead, I would not stay on. I would work for them for six months and would then leave. My early experience of selling and staying on as an employee had not been good. I had no intention of going through that again.

Perhaps someone, or something, was telling me it was time to retire gracefully.

What about the people? I knew Encription was at a stage where it was sound, and had massive potential. I also knew I was not the person to fully realise that potential. James and Emmie might be.

I needed time to think, but I didn't have that much time. On the call BlackBerry had made it clear that if this deal was going to happen, then it needed to happen quickly. They wanted to complete a deal no later than December that year. It was now July.

After much discussion we decided to pursue it. The due diligence needed to be conducted in complete secrecy. There were two people in Encription who would have to give input, and provide information; Dawn, our HR manager, and Diane, who was now our full-time accountant. They needed to be told.

BlackBerry were bringing a due diligence team over. We would put them up in the hotel where we had board meetings and all questioning would go on in a private room in the hotel.

The due diligence team would need to visit the offices. We would arrange that at seven o'clock in the evening when there was no one there. Paddy would have to fly over, as the offer included the Irish business.

I knew from past experience that this was going to be a time-consuming exercise, which may come to nothing. In the meantime, we had to be careful that we did not neglect the day-to-day business.

They would want copies of all employee contracts, client agreements, accounts and payroll; in fact, everything and anything concerning the company, its assets and its liabilities.

If we gave any incorrect information, or misled them in any way, they would be able to contractually come back to us, post-sale, and demand recompense. We already knew that if the sale went ahead they would keep a percentage of the consideration back. This amount of retention would be paid in full after eighteen months, providing everything had been as we had declared. If anything came to light that we had not declared, then BlackBerry could deduct the equivalent amount from the retention.

The first meeting of the due diligence team was friendly but intense. There were nine people from BlackBerry, including technical, financial, human resources and contracts. Two of the team had been employees of companies that BlackBerry had recently acquired, so they knew what we were going through. One of them was very aggressive in their questioning.

Even though I had been through due diligence several times before, and I knew what to expect, it still doesn't change the amount of digging that has to be done and the number of long-lost details and documents that need to be found; some of which you never had in the first place. The due diligence lasted five long days and nights but was not yet complete. Even after the due diligence team had left there were still more questions to be answered.

Over the previous three years we had been developing some new products. It had always been my intention that we would only deliver penetration testing, but we had since then diversified into training and forensics.

In doing so we had seen a need for products that would allow users to run their own automated vulnerability tests. Whilst they would have a penetration test every year, which would highlight any vulnerabilities and provide remediation advice, in the period between penetration tests, new vulnerabilities would be introduced. These vulnerabilities would not be found until the next penetration test, leaving the organisation and its IT at risk.

Additionally, for Encription, selling products such as the scanners, which run on a more regular basis, would generate contracted income, which selling services can only do to a limited extent.

There were three products we had developed: the internal scanner, which was run by the client on their own servers; the external scanner, which was run from Encription's servers over the Internet and tested the clients' IT systems; and a website scanner, which was also run from Encription's offices and examined the security of a website on a daily basis. There was also a new product, which we were still developing, which we called Encriptor.

The scanners were aimed at medium to large companies and allowed their IT departments to select which IT assets they wanted to check for security vulnerabilities, and with what frequency, which could be daily.

The scanners were updated on a regular basis, usually when a new vulnerability had been identified. Vulnerability scanning is a very good interim test, but because it is automated it does not use the human logic that is used in a full penetration test. The human tester may identify a vulnerability but ignore it because of other defences which are in place, which will prevent the vulnerability from being exploited. Automated scanners do not have this human logic.

The scanners did give up-to-date assurance that IT security was being monitored on a regular basis. The users of the scanners needed to licence a piece of third-party software that was quite expensive, but still cost considerably less than a manual penetration test.

Encriptor was aimed at smaller users who found the cost of the third-party licence too expensive. We had spent a lot of time and invested a substantial amount of money in developing it, but we saw a large potential market.

BlackBerry carried out their due diligence. They were keen to have a demonstration of all three products, which we did, post the five days of due diligence, via a transatlantic video conference.

Conversations between us went on for some time, our staff being unware as to what was happening in the background.

Paddy thought we were selling too soon.

In the meantime, BlackBerry had been pursuing other acquisition targets; one in particular was worth $425 million. The acquisition of this company would delay our negotiations.

Around September time, BlackBerry came back to us with a revised offer. The offer, as expected, consisted of the majority of the consideration up front, but with a percentage being held back for eighteen months in case there were any skeletons in the cupboard.

They did not want the scanners or Encriptor. They said it was not their market. As a result, they would reduce the offer price. Campbell and I could keep the rights to the scanners and Encriptor; they would be contractually referred to as the "Excluded Assets".

The price they offered was still acceptable, and more than we had expected. It was agreed that Campbell would be employed by BlackBerry. He would sign a three-year contract. He would not be able to get involved in the Excluded Assets. I was going to retire when I had completed my six-month contract. I didn't have the appetite for a new venture.

On 19 February 2016 we sold Encription.

I should have been overjoyed as the very large bank transfer went into my account, but I wasn't. I was worried about the staff, and especially Emmie and James, who would remain as employees. I was also very aware that when I had sold in the past and having a large amount of money was new to me, I had invested in some unwise investments. I had lost a lot of money.

I was older and wiser now. I had been making a good living through Encription and was at a stage in life where experiences were far more important to me than material things. We had a nice house, and I was done with flashy cars and the cost of keeping them. Not to mention how fast they lost money. There was nothing I wanted. I had had several months in which to think about what I would do with the money, if the sale went ahead. I had decided that I would simply put it into savings accounts that would provide an income, although with the bank rate so pitifully low, it wasn't going to be substantial. I would be eating into capital. But I would be able to live well on it for a long time.

One of my traits as a control freak was that I could become impatient if something was not done properly. As an example, I hated airports. I always felt that there must be a better way of managing the people traffic, rather than treating them like cattle who were about to go to slaughter. It was because of this feeling, and wanting experiences, that I had decided some time ago that, if I could afford it, I would fly by private jet. Probably not all of the time, but at least once. Now I had money and some spare time, I would do it. This would fit in well with Ann's dad, Alan, who at ninety-two was determined that he wanted to visit Ireland once more before he died. He had had a stroke eighteen months previously which had left him with mobility problems, so any thought of going by a commercial airline and battling with airports was out of the question, but a private jet would work well.

I organised a seven-seater jet, even though there would only be three of us. It would fly from Gloucester Airport to Waterford. I was more excited than anyone. On the day, it could not have been easier.

We drove straight up to the steps of the aircraft where one of the two pilots helped Alan up the short steps into the cabin. Our car was driven away and kept in a hangar ready for our return. Alan settled himself into the luxurious cream leather seat as though he did this all of the time. No queues, even to take off. We decided. I had decided what time we would fly both going and on our return.

As we took off there were smiles all around. Once fully airborne, one of the pilots came and offered us both food and drink. This was the way to live. The flight was only thirty minutes. Our longest wait was at Waterford Airport where we had to circle a few times whilst the ground staff frightened the many birds from the runway; we were the only plane. Now I knew why I preferred experiences.

In a very short space of time I had gone from being totally involved in business to being unemployed; at least, I would be in six months' time, when my contract ended.

Those six months were like a prison sentence which seemed as though it would never end. There was nothing wrong with BlackBerry. It was inevitable that they would do things differently. It just proved to me that I really was unemployable.

On Friday 15 July 2016, after fifty years in IT, I finished my working life.

I knew that I would miss it: the day-to-day challenges; the thrill of getting new business. The real truth and loss only hit me sometime later.

When we had moved into Encription House I had spent quite a lot of money, not to mention time and effort in its design. This included chrome signage both at the front and the rear of the building. The letters were very large and made it clear that Encription IT Security lived here. Every time I drove past in the morning that sign made me proud.

One morning, two weeks after I had retired, I came past Encription House to see workmen on a small hoist removing my signage and replacing it with, what I considered to be, a brash BlackBerry sign.

THE EPILOGUE

I loved all of my family dearly. I just wanted everything to be right for them. I wanted to be able to wave a magic wand and make everything better, but don't we all? In the absence of a wand I showed my love materialistically, when what I should have done was just give them the love and attention that they wanted and deserved. But I didn't know how to. It was something I needed to learn.

Ann had a very good saying. It was, "You are only as happy as your unhappiest child". This was certainly the case.

I had hidden behind my work for fifty years. In some ways, she was my mistress. I knew I could never be an employee because I needed to be in control, to be the boss. And at my age, who would employ me, anyway? I thought about non-executive directorships, but was too lethargic to do anything about it, and I would not be in charge.

I needed recognition and power. Having sold the business I no longer had this. I had gone from full-on to empty days with no purpose, no direction, and at times no meaning. All I had was money, and it didn't mean anything.

Having walked the *Camino*, Ann and I had continued to walk almost daily, driven by a demanding Pointer dog who wanted a lot of exercise. I loved walking on my own with the dog. She knew more of my feelings than anyone. We would do long walks, taking in the changing seasons, the quietness and peacefulness of the 2,000 acres of forest nearby. This was close to the happiness I craved.

In my absence, whilst working, Ann had created her own routine, her own circle of friends and things to do. Her dad needed a lot of attention, and certainly a daily visit from Ann. She was golden to him. He now had carers coming in four times every day, but he still needed the loving support of his only child. I could of course become part of that routine, and to an extent I did, but it did not fulfil me. I wasn't good at it, and it wasn't what I wanted.

We had booked some holidays long before the approach from BlackBerry. The first one took place at the end of my contract with BlackBerry. It was a blessing in disguise because it meant that as soon as I retired I had something to do, something to look forward to. We booked several other holidays including to India, Japan and Australia. They were a distraction from the boredom and discontentment of retirement.

I thought about buying a new car. I didn't need one, but it was something to do. A Bentley? A Range Rover? A Tesla?

I had spent money with almost gay abandon after the previous sales of my businesses, but I had learned lessons. I was probably not going to earn a wage again. What we had had to last us and keep us into old age. The money needed investing carefully and not squandering on things that were not needed, unless of course it was for Ann, Emmie and James or any of the grandchildren.

The unhappiness continued, although, over time, I did find myself more relaxed, including amongst friends. Previously I had always had work and work problems in the back of my mind, which were a distraction.

Drink was another threat. I had been drinking from about the age of sixteen and had always been lucky enough to know when I had had enough and to stop. Drink can make things that are a problem seem less of a problem. This can certainly be the case if, as they often were with me, it is a perceived rather than a real problem. I enjoy drinking. It is the one time when I become relaxed enough to be that person in the pub or restaurant laughing at the inane or innocent comment. Once I had retired I could see the danger signals. When bored it was easy to think of going for a drink. My awareness of this meant that I only drank when I really wanted to and not because it took away the boredom.

It took me until March of 2017, seven months after I had retired, to start feeling happy again; to be more positive and outgoing. I got involved in a few church projects, started brushing up on my Spanish, and read several Spanish novels, although somewhat slowly, but it passed the time, and certainly improved my vocabulary.

Having sold our apartment in Spain a few years previously, Ann and I were now thinking about buying another one, perhaps spending more time out there. I needed to be in a better place mentally before I took that step. I was also reticent to spend the sort of money that would be needed

Writing this book certainly helped. It was very slow at times, often neglected for weeks on end, but I would always return to it, especially on days when I was bored. It was perhaps the counselling I needed. My own self-counselling; a way of making me put things, and my life in particular, into perspective; to see things more positively, and be happy.

The book made me look at the past: what I had gone through; what I had achieved; where I was now. It was both therapeutic and cathartic.

More and more I began to appreciate what I had got; not just money, but my family and life in general. How lucky I was.

I could be walking along the street or be in a supermarket. I would see someone, perhaps stacking shelves, and wonder if they had missed their own opportunities; how happy they were with their life; if they might have the talent to become a trainee penetration tester.

I have very much become a house-husband. I even know how to use the washing machine and tumble dryer, which I didn't before.

Ann and I do more things together.

I think about starting a business again, but I don't want the twenty-four-seven commitment. If I did it I would employ as few people as possible. Preferably none. We would probably make widgets. Something that was uncomplicated and couldn't go wrong.

I knew I was fooling myself. I didn't do simple or uncomplicated.

So many people said to me, 'What are you going to do next? What's your next venture? You will never retire.'

Was this it? Was I finally retired? Was I finished?

How did I get here???????

I still had the scanners and Encriptor. The Excluded Assets.

Let's wait and see.